The Irish in Newfoundland

1600 - 1900

Their Trials, Tribulations and

Triumphs

by

Mike McCarthy

The Irish in Newfoundland

1600 - 1900

Their Trials, Tribulations and
Triumphs

by
Mike McCarthy

St. John's, Newfoundland
1999

© 1999, Michael McCarthy

The Canada Council | Le Conseil des Arts
for the arts | du Canada
since 1957 | depuis 1957

We acknowledge the support of The Canada Council for the Arts for our
publishing program.
The publisher acknowledges the financial contribution of the
*Department of Tourism and Culture, Government of Newfoundland and
Labrador,* which has helped make this publication possible.
We acknowledge the financial support of the Department for Canadian Heri-
tage for our publishing program.

Cover Art and Design:
Boyd Chubbs

∞ Printed on acid-free paper

Published by
CREATIVE BOOK PUBLISHING

a division of 10366 Newfoundland Limited

a Robinson-Blackmore Printing & Publishing associated company

P.O. Box 8660, St. John's, Newfoundland A1B 3T7

First printing, March 1999

Second printing, May 1999

Third printing, January 2000

Printed in Canada by:

ROBINSON-BLACKMORE PRINTING & PUBLISHING

Canadian Cataloguing in Publication Data

McCarthy, Michael J., 1932-

   The Irish in Newfoundland 1600-1900

   Includes bibliographical references and index.
   ISBN 1-894294-04-1

1. Irish — Newfoundland — History.
2. Irish Canadians — Newfoundland — History.   I. Title.

FC220.I6M32   1999   971.8'0049162   C99-950041-4
F1125.I6M32   1999

Dedication

To my wife Anna, son Michael, daughter Karen and to all the early Irish Pioneers, including my paternal ancestor, Timothy McCarthy, who braved the perils of an Atlantic crossing to seek a better life in a new land.

Young Irish Immigrant

Table of Contents

Seventeenth century settler's house in Newfoundland

Preface

It is perhaps very appropriate that the great oil field off the coast of Newfoundland has been named "Hibernia", for legend has it that a group of Irish monks led by Saint Brendan were the first Europeans to visit our shores. Although many centuries passed before the Irish returned to Newfoundland, they did come again and since the early 17th century have played an important, if sometimes stormy part, in shaping the course of Newfoundland history.

Mistrusted by their English masters because of their race and religion, they nevertheless soon established themselves, and before long respectable lower middle class Irish were keeping shops and taverns and acting as agents for British fishing firms.

Drink, especially the potent "Flip"—a mixture of rum and spruce beer—was often the undoing of the young Irish fishermen who first came to Newfoundland. This led to faction fights that sometimes ended in death. Unfortunately few of the good deeds of the Irish were recorded, but their appearances in court make for lively reading.

Persecuted for practising their Roman Catholic faith, they worshiped in secret, until Governor Campbell's edict of 1784. In 1828 they came of age politically when all religious restrictions were relaxed. Soon, led by their Irish born bishop, Michael Anthony Fleming O.F., they learned the fine art of politics and became a force to be reckoned with. In 1855, Philip Francis Little, a Prince Edward Island man of Irish ancestry, became the first Prime Minister of the colony of Newfoundland. In 1917, Sir Edward Morris, the 12th Prime Minister of Newfoundland, was created Baron Morris. He was the first and only Newfoundlander of Irish ancestry to receive such an honour.

Philip Francis Little
First Prime Minister of Newfoundland
under Responsible Government

Acknowledgements

Edgar Blundon
Frank Galgay
F. Burnham Gill
Joe Kinsella
Alice Lannon
Mrs. Queen Maloney
The late Dr. Keith Matthews
The Late Msgr. J. O'Brien
Captain Joseph Prim
Dr. Otto Tucker
The staff of the Newfoundland Historical Society office.
The Staff of the Newfoundland Section of the Newfoundland
    Provincial Library
The staff of the Newfoundland Provincial Archives.

*Early 17th century British ship of the type which brought
the Irish Princess to Carbonear*

Chapter One

The First Irish Connections

The Voyage of Saint Brendan:

The first mention of an Irish connection with Newfoundland is the legendary tale of the voyage of Saint Brendan. Saint Brendan was an Irish monk who was born in 484 near Tralee, Ireland, and died at Annaghdown in 577. According to a 10th century manuscript, Saint Brendan and a band of monks sailed westward in the sixth century from their monastery near Brandon Hill, Kerry in search of new lands. They returned after a voyage of seven years and reported having discovered a region covered with luxuriant vegetation.[1] As a result of this journey, Saint Brendan was afterwards referred to as the "Voyager." The story of Saint Brendan's voyage was so popular in the 15th century it was one of the first books published in English by William Caxton. There is also a tradition from Iceland that when the Norsemen came to North America in the ninth century they found an Irish colony already established there.[2]

---

1 *New Catholic Dictionary*, Vatican Edition, New York, 1929 p.139
2 Howley, M.F. Rt. Rev., *Ecclesiastical History of Nfld.*, Boston, 1888,p. 40.

In 1977, Timothy Severin and three crewmen recreated the voyage of Saint Brendan using a wooden frame boat covered with leather and constructed in the manner of a 6th century craft. They successfully crossed the Atlantic and landed at Peckford Island, on the "Straight Shore" of Newfoundland. This voyage, completed on June 26, 1977, proved that the 6th century voyage of Saint Brendan was indeed possible, and that Newfoundland would most likely have been the land he discovered.

The Legend of the Irish Princess of Carbonear:

Another early legend of an Irish presence in Newfoundland is the story of Shelia Nagueria, the Irish princess who settled in the Carbonear area in the first decade of the seventeenth century. According to a strong local tradition the ship on which she was travelling from Ireland to attend a convent school in France was captured by a Dutch warship and she was taken prisoner. She was rescued by Peter Easton, then an English naval captain. Easton's ship was bound for Newfoundland and the Irish Princess went with him. On the way over she fell in love with and married Gilbert Pike, Easton's second in command. On reaching Newfoundland, Pike settled with his new wife in Bristol's Hope, but later moved to Carbonear. There are many stories about the Irish Princess, how she nursed the sick and took command in times of danger, but unfortunately there is no written record to verify the legend.

Lord Falkland's Appeal for Irish Settlers for Newfoundland:

The first active recruitment of Irish settlers for Newfoundland came in 1623, when Lord Falkland, the Lord Deputy of Ireland, who was planning to found a colony at Renews, had a book published in Dublin inviting Irishmen to participate in his venture. According to Robert Hayman, the 17th century Harbour Grace poet, some of Falkland's settlers came, but there is nothing to indicate that they were Irish.[1] However, there is an old oral tradition handed down in St. Mary's Bay that the original settlers of that area were Irish settlers brought out by Lord Falkland for the Renews colony. After the failure of the Falkland colony they were hounded from the Renews area and sought sanctuary in St. Mary's Bay.[2]

First Mention of an Irish Settler:

The first reference to an Irish settler in Newfoundland was to a Mr. Russell, who was reported living in St. Mary's. In 1662, a warrant was issued for his arrest for non-payment of rent to Governor Pearce at Ferryland. The warrant was never served as John Matthews, who was sent to serve it, was taken prisoner by a French Captain who told him that all of southern Newfoundland now belonged to the king of France. Matthews later escaped and made his way back to Ferryland.[3] There is no further record of Mr. Russell's stay in St. Mary's. In fact, all reports both from the English and French colonial records indicate that Trepassey, which had both English and French inhabitants, was the only settled community in St. Mary's Bay prior to the Treaty of Utrecht in 1713.

Beginning of Irish Trade With Newfoundland:

There seems to have been little Irish involvement in the Newfoundland fishery until the second half of the seventeenth century. However, in 1675 it was reported that there were Irish settlers living at Ireland's Eye, Trinity Bay.[4] There is also some evidence of trade between Irish merchants and

1 Cell, Gillian, *English Enterprise in Newfoundland*, Toronto, 1969, p.90.
2 English, L.E.F., *Historic Newfoundland*, Montreal, 1957, p.20.
3 Prowse, D.W., *A History of Newfoundland*, London, 1896, p.179
  Rogers, J.D., *A Historical Geography of the British Colonies*, volume, V Part 1V, Newfoundland, Oxford, 1911, p.79
4 Nemec, Thomas, "Irish Immigration to Newfoundland", *Newfoundland Quarterly*, July, 1972, p.17.

the French colony at Placentia, for in 1676 John Aylrod, an Irish merchant from Waterford, gave an account of the French colony after a trading visit there.[1]

In 1679, five sack ships from Ireland were reported in Newfoundland; three from Waterford, one from Yougal and one from Dublin. In 1681, it was reported that Irish traders were bringing goods and:

> A great many women passengers which they sell for sevts a little after their coming they marry among fishermen that live with the planters & being extreamly poor contract such debts as they are not able to pay.[2]

After 1690, the troubled times in Ireland forced many of its young men to flee the country and when the Newfoundland fishing convoy stopped at Waterford to pick up provisions, there were plenty of "Irish Youngsters" willing to serve for two summers and a winter in the Newfoundland fishery. Many of them married planters' daughters and never returned to Ireland.

Pere Baudoin's Account of Irish Servants in Newfoundland:

By 1696, there was a growing Irish presence in various Newfoundland communities. Pere Baudoin, the Recollet Father who accompanied D'Iberville on his attacks on the English settlements in the fall of 1696, reported the capture of eight Irish servants at Brigus. These servants, he wrote, were treated by their English masters like slaves. He went on to say that some of the Irish servants joined the French in their attack on the English settlements and that three Irishmen were captured by the English at Carbonear. At Heart's Content, an Irishman had been put in charge of the town's

---

1   Prowse, D.J., History of Newfoundland, London, 1895, p. 206.
2   CO1/47 f. 115.

defences, but surrendered without a fight as soon as D'Iberville and his Indians arrived. It is interesting to note that while the English agreed during a prisoner exchange to one English prisoner for one French prisoner, they demanded three Irishmen for each French prisoner that they released.[1]

Dangers From Irish Population:

In 1705, the naval officer at St. John's warned that care should be taken to control the growing Irish population in Newfoundland:

> Of the Irish resideing in the Country for they by our dialy Experience have proved very detrimental to the Govermt. here ffore when the Enemy makes any Incursion upon us they doe take up armes and informe our Enemy And prove very treacherous and our greatest Enemy.[2]

The Presence of Irish Soldiers:

There were also Irish soldiers in the regiment guarding the fort in St. John's during the fall of 1708. In the early hours of the morning of December 21, 1708, the sentry on night duty was an Irishman and there was some suspicion that he let the French enter the fort before giving an alarm. However, this could not be proved as the man claimed he had tried to give the alarm by firing his musket, but it had mis-fired.

A letter dated December 1, 1711, from Captain Jos. Crow, the commodore of the Newfoundland convoy gives the number of English planters residing in the island as 2281. He did not report the presence of Irish servants, but did write that some of the train oil produced by the planters was sold to sack ships that came from Ireland. In the same year another report stated that there were factors for Irish mer-

1 Howley, M.F. Rt. Rev. *Ecclestical History of Newfoundland,*, p.179.
2 CO 194/3 f.424

chants residing in St. John's. In 1715, it was reported that there were 20 ships from Ireland in Newfoundland.

The Irish population of Newfoundland greatly increased after 1713, when the French colonies in Newfoundland were ceded to the English. Colonel Moody, who had been appointed Lieutenant Governor of Placentia, under the jurisdiction of the Governor of Nova Scotia, brought out four Irish regiments to man the fort there. At the end of their tour of duty many of these Irishmen remained in the Placentia area and later settled in a number of communities along the Southern Shore and in Placentia Bay.

Among the more famous of the descendants of one of these Irish Soldiers from Placentia was the prophet Richards Brothers. His father, William Brothers, married a girl from Island Cove and left Placentia to settle at Clam Cove near Cape Race. He later moved his family to Admiral's Cove (Port Kirwin), where some of his descendants still live. At Admiral's Cove he leased the de Glanwell plantation from John Mudge in 1752 and laid out vast sums of money to improve the plantation.[1]

His famous son, Richard, was born at Admiral's Cove around 1757. He joined the British navy and rose to the rank of Lieutenant. Then he began to have visions and announced that he was God's nephew. He also laid claim to the throne of England and as a result was locked up in an asylum in 1795. He was released under a kind of house arrest to one of his friends in 1795, where he remained until his death in 1824.

The Petty Harbour Murder, 1720:

In 1720, the number of Irish servants staying over the winter became a concern to the English settlers after an Irish servant stabbed his master, Thomas Ford, in his own house in Petty Harbour. Ford died from the stab wounds and the servant

---

1   Galgay, Frank, *A Pilgrimage of Faith*, St. John's, 1983, p.60.

was taken into custody on orders from William Kean, a St. John's merchant and commissioner of a special court convened at St. John's in 1719. Kean inherited Ford's property at Petty Harbour and he arranged at his own expense to send the Irish servant to England to stand trial at Exeter. Judge Prowse, a 19th century Newfoundland historian, described Ford as a violent man and the "self appointed governor" of Petty Harbour. As a direct result of this incident at Petty Harbour, Captain Percy R. N. in his report for 1720 warned of the danger of the growing Irish population in Newfoundland.

In the spring of 1721 a number of Petty Harbour planters complained to the governor that during the winter season they lived in fear of their idle servants. They requested that merchants at St. John's like William Kean be given the authority to hold courts and punish persons who committed crimes during the absence of the Fishing Admirals and the naval officers.[1] Nothing was done until 1729, when Newfoundland got its first governor with authority to appoint district magistrates who would reside in the island all year round. However, all persons accused of capital crimes still had to be sent to England for trial. The first court of Oyer and Terminer with authority to try capital crimes was not established until 1750.

Irish Trade with Newfoundland:

Because of restrictive Irish export trade laws passed by the English Parliament, dairy produce in Ireland could be purchased much more cheaply than in England. As a result the fishing convoys on their outward voyage to Newfoundland usually put into the ports of Waterford and Cork to take on their food supplies. In fact, by 1742, out of 958 firkins of butter imported into Newfoundland, 883 were supplied by the merchants of Waterford and Cork. As a result of this trade

---

1 C.O. 194/7, p. 22.

the number of Irish servants recruited for the Newfoundland fishery continued to grow and the Irish population of Newfoundland increase fourfold between 1713 and 1756. A census taken in the town of St. Mary's in 1732 showed a total resident population of 38, 10 of whom were male Irish servants.

In 1752 the Irish in Newfoundland numbered about 3,000 and constituted half of the population. The 1753 population for various Newfoundland communities gave the number of English and Irish inhabitants at each location.

Community	English	Irish
St. John's, Quidi Vidi, Torbay	454	669
Bay Bulls Willey Bay Toad's Cove	206	395
Fermeuse	50	68
Ferryland	120 ·	130
Renews	82	100
Old Perlican	100	166
Trinity Bay and Bonavista	513	700
Carbonear and Musquito	222	400
Bay de Verde	69	59
	1,816	2,687[1]

A census for St. Mary's in 1754 shows the total population of that community had grown to 383 persons which included 100 male Irish servants, 6 female Irish servants and 20 children of Irish parents.

During the winter there was little employment and much heavy drinking. As a result many of the Irish servants lived, according to the English authorities in "idleness, drunkness and disorder."[2] This became a cause of concern to Lord Vere

1 C.O. 194: 13
2 Gunn Geretrude, *The Political History of Newfoundland*, Toronto 1966, p. 8

Beauclerk in 1728 and was later reiterated by Governor Clinton in 1731 and Governor Byng in 1743.[1]

The Oath of Allegiance and Abjuration:

In 1747, and again in 1749, Governors Rodney and Drake expressed alarm at the rapid growth of the Irish population in Newfoundland. As Bonnie Prince Charlie's rebellion of 1745 had just ended, they were especially concerned that the Irish Roman Catholics in Newfoundland refused to take an oath of allegiance to the reigning monarch of the House of Hanover. The oath was unacceptable to the Irish, because after swearing allegiance to the House of Hanover, the person also had to abjure the Roman Catholic doctrine of transubstantiation. The oath read:

> I (name of person taking the oath) do declare that I do not believe there is any transubstantation in the sacrament of the Lord's Supper, or in any element of bread or wine, at or after the consecration thereof, by any persons whatsoever. So help me God.[2]

They refusal to take this oath was taken as evidence that the person concerned was a supporter of Bonnie Prince Charles and the Stuart cause. In 1750, Governor Drake made this report on the Irish:

> A great number of Irish papist remain in the country during the winter to the great prejudice and dread of the inhabitants, and if timely measures cannot be taken to prevent the masters of ships bringing with them such numbers yearly, it may be of the greatest prejudice to the Trade in general, as they are notoriously disaffected to the govern-

---

1   Rogers, J.D., *Historical Geography of the British Colonies*,
    Volume V,-Part 1V, Oxford, 1911, p. 112.
2   Court Records of Placentia, Manuscript, 1762.

ment, all of them refusing to take the oath of allegiance
when tendered to them. The majority of the inhabitants to
the Southward of St. John's are Papists but to the North-
ward very few. The numbers of Papists at St. John's last year
was 600, men, women and children, but I could get no
exact account of the numbers in other ports, but it is
generally contended that one fourth part of the inhabitants
are Irish papists.[1]

Irish Bringing Children From Newfoundland to Ireland for Baptism:

As there were no resident priests in Newfoundland, some of
the Irish brought their children home to Ireland for baptism.
For instance the church records for St. Patrick's church in
Waterford show that between 1730-1780, 28 children born of
Irish parents in Newfoundland were brought back to St.
Patrick's for baptism.

Irish Servant Girls in St. John's:

By 1750, we have evidence from the early court records of
Irish girls serving as domestic servants in St. John's. One of
these was Catherine Keef who served in the house of William
Gillmore. On the afternoon of August 19, 1750, Catherine
became aware that something strange was going on when her
mistress ordered her to clean the cooking pot. Catherine told
Mrs Gillmore that there was chowder in the pot for supper,
but Mrs Gillmore told her to clean the pot as she expected
company. Later two Scotsmen from the brig *Diamond* came
in to collect some sewing Mrs Gillmore had done for them.
They gave Catherine a shilling to go get some rum, and her
mistress told her to fetch it from Kate Tybol's. She returned
with the rum and found four soldiers had also come to
supper. Catherine then went out again for she didn't like
being around Richard Sutcliff, one of the soldiers whom she

---

1   C.O. 194/25, p. 24.

knew, for he was always proposing indecent things to her. She returned and went to bed when the visitors had all gone.

Later that night the four soldiers came back and knocked at Gillmore's window. His wife begged him not to let them in as they would be harbouring thieves. In court on September 7, Catherine gave the following evidence about the subsequent events of the night:

> Gillmore then struck his wife on her ribs, called her a bitch, got up and let the said persons into the house where they stayed till about dawning and she heard them cutting something which by the cutting seemed to be victuals. In the morning James Forrister brought a knife and asked Margaret Gillmore if it was hers, she answered she had a knife but could not be certain, but carried it to her husband who said it was his, the said Forrister them told him he would come to hurt if the knife was his for it was the knife which the cow had been killed with last night. The said Gillmore replied if it had killed twenty cows, the knife was his. Then Forrister went away and carried the knife with him, when Margaret Gillmore began to cry saying to her husband he had brought her to shame and disgrace all on account of liquor, then the said Gillmore got out of bed took some fresh beef out of a pork casque and carried it to a pile of wood in the garden where he hid it, then came to this deponent and said, Katye if this thing should be known, you can take your oath that you did not see me out of my bed for the night, this deponent replied that she could take her oath no further than that she saw him twice in the night, once when she saw him at supper and once to let the above persons into the house, then she said Gillmore went and put some stones over part of the beef which was hid in the well and asked this deponent to put the pork casque over the well in order to hide the beef which she did and further this deponent sayeth not.[1]

1 .Ibid

At the trial two of the soldiers, Mick Hayes and George Gardner, gave evidence against their companions and William Gillmore and escaped punishment. Catherine, although she had been involved in hiding the beef, was not charged with having any part in the crime. David Williams, Richard Sutcliff and William Gillmore were sentenced to be hanged. However, Williams and Sutcliff were recommended to the governor for mercy, but Gillmore received the death penalty.

Sale of Property Owned by Irish Widow:

By the mid-eighteenth century some Irish persons held property in St. John's and the sale of a piece of property by an Irish woman living in Waterford, Ireland took place on September 17, 1750. The deed was recorded in the Governor's Letterbook.

> Margaret Reardon—otherwise known as Whelan's widow—now living in the city of Waterford, Ireland for four pounds eleven shillings sold to Ed. Cockran of St. John's, a half meadow near Freshwater on the north side of the same town situated in Newfoundland. The sale was registered by order of the governor.[1]

By the middle of the 18th, century some Irish settlers had become prominent citizens in their community. Dan Murphy of Renews was a leading citizen of that town, and served on a jury in 1752. He had considerable property in the community and his boundaries were defined as:

> The water side, flakes east and west 244 ft., north and south 200 ft., abounded by the widow Power's Room and ship's Room and back up to Maurice Cunningham's house to

---

1 *Colonial Letterbook* Volume 1, September 17, 1750.

Boat Cove with the stores, flakes and dwelling house and
all enclosures belonging to him.[1]

In 1753, Mary Clarke, Timothy O'Keefe, Thomas Kennedy and Edward McCarthroy of Placentia were issued li-
cences to keep public houses and at St. John's William
Murphy was serving as assistant constable. At Harbour Grace,
Felix McCarthy had two ships—the *Shamrock* and *Francis &
Elizabeth*—and his own fishing crew. As well, he served as
agent for several English firms in carrying on their business
in Newfoundland.

---

1 *Colonial Letterbook* Volume 11, p.123.

17th century Newfoundland fishing stage

Chapter Two

Justice For the Newfoundland Irish

The Irish servants who first came to Newfoundland found little justice when they were oppressed by their masters. The first magistrates appointed in Newfoundland in 1729 were merchants, and like the fishing admirals who still claimed legal jurisdiction in all fishery matters, they were often personally involved in the cases of debts and non payment of wages and other civil actions that came before them. Capital crimes did not come under the jurisdiction of either the Fishing Admirals or the local magistrates until 1741 and until that date these crimes had to be tried in England.

At first the Irish accepted the harsh judgements of the Fishing Admirals and magistrates, but towards the middle of the 18th century they began to take their complaints of ill treatment and non payment of wages to the governor, or the naval officers who acted as his surrogate. At this level, they found that they could often obtain the justice denied them in the local courts. One of the earliest recorded cases of Irish fishermen appealing to the governor for justice was in 1749.

Moreen and Careen's Appeal to the Governor:

One of the first recorded appeals to the governor came from Michael Mooren and David Careen, two Irish servants at

Carbonear. In the late summer of 1749, feeling they had been denied justice in their local court, they petitioned the governor for redress against the cruel treatment they had received from their master, John Pike. They claimed that on Pike's orders, his servants Thomas Fling, James Poor, Edmund Redman and George Pierce had seized both Mooreen and Careen, and dragged them aboard a galley belonging to Pike which was anchored in Carbonear Harbour. Here they were stripped and tied to the vessel's shrouds. Then Moreen received 40 lashes and Careen 80. This was done, the two men claimed, without any provocation on their part. Governor Rodney made inquiries and then ordered Pike and his servants to appear in court to answer for their actions. When they defied the governor's order and did not appear in court he issued a warrant for their arrest and on September 18, 1750, sent a stiff letter to the local Justices of the Peace at Carbonear on their neglect of duty:

> Your behaviour in this affair has obliged me to reprimand you in this manner, for remember gentlemen I am sent to administer justice to rich and poor alike without favour or partiality. You likewise by the oath you have taken as Justices of the Peace are obliged to do the same, in neglect of which you will not only forswear yourself but be liable to be severely punished according to law, AND YOU MAY DEPEND UPON IT I AM NOT TO BE TRIFLED WITH IN THE EXECUTION OF MY OFFICE[1]

The Carbonear magistrates did their duty this time and Pike appeared in court, where he was found guilty and ordered to pay damages of 15 and 20 pounds to Moreen and Careen respectively.

---

1 *Colonial Letterbook*, Volume 1, September 18, 1849.

In 1753, the Carbonear Justices of the Peace again neglected to act on a complaint made by Ed Quinlan, Pat Roach, Nat Barry and Ed Maher that John Gifford of Carbonear refused to pay the wages due to them from their master James Howell. Gifford had signed a note to pay the balance due in bills of exchange. Quinlan and his companions appealed to the governor who ordered Gifford to make the payment.

In a similar case at Placentia in 1754 where a local planter took the law into his own hands, the governor again warned the magistrate there to be more careful in his administration of juctice. In this case, a Captain Phippard, who was not a magistrate, had called together a court and under his own signature issued a warrant giving his men authority to seize the plantation of a planter named Dennis. He then sent his armed servants who, after dragging Dennis out of his house, took full possession. Dennis complained to the governor who issued this warning to William Bruce, the senior magistrate at Placentia.

> I am suprised that you as a magistrate will allow such illegal and barbarous proceedings, which must consequently be the ruin of many honest and useful subjects.

The governor also sent a naval officer to examine into Phippard's actions. Phippard was found guilty and Dennis's property was restored to him.

Unjust Irish Masters:

Between the years 1750-55 an ever increasing number of Irishmen appeared in the surrogate or naval officer's courts, usually seeking redress from the unjust oppression of their masters, or that the wages due them be paid as well as their passage back to Ireland. One of the interesting facts that appear from these court cases is that some Irish servants had risen to become masters themselves. However, as masters the Irish could be as cruel and unjust in their treatment of servants as the English masters. An example of this appears in the case of John Flannigan of St. John's. In 1753 he petitioned the court against his master, Thomas Flannigan, for non payment of wages and his passage home. Again the governor ruled in favour of the servant.

In a similar manner on August 29, 1780, Patrick Dawson, a servant to John Nagle of Petty Harbour, found out what it was like to have a suspicious Irish master. Dawson was spreading out fish when he saw a dog running across the flake with a piece of beef in his mouth. Dawson caught the dog and took away the meat. He was on his way to return it to the cook room when John Nagle came up and accused him of stealing the beef. Nagle dismissed Dawson on the spot and even refused to pay his wages for the time he had worked for him. Dawson appealed his dismissal and Nagle was ordered to take him back and pay him for the time he had worked.

A Scam to Avoid Paying for Passage to Placentia:

However, sometimes the appeals by Irish servants to the governor and Surrogate Court were proven false. At Placentia in 1753, William Bryan, Michael Sullivan, Daniel King, Edward King, and John Byran petitioned the Surrogate Court at Placentia against the cruel treatment they had received from the Captain of the brig that had brought them to Placentia. In an investigation by the naval officer, the testimony of Captain Hogg of the brig was backed up by Richard Welsh, a Placentia merchant who had come over on the same ship. The story was proved false. The court ordered that enough money be deducted from their wages to pay the men's passage back home.

Old Grievances:

Sometimes the Irish brought their grievances from the Old World to the New. This was the case in 1750, when Patrick Poor (Power), while fishing off Cape St. Francis, threw a rock and broke the arm of Thomas Parr who was fishing in a boat nearby. Parr had given no cause for such an attack. As he threw the stone Poor cried out in a loud voice, "Damn you, the king and your country!" Parr took Poor to court on a charge of assault and loss of wages. The case came to the governor's attention and he ordered Poor to pay Parr damages for his lost wages.[1]

Women Troubles:

By 1750, some of the Irish servants and soldiers were appearing in court charged with fighting over or molesting women. There were few women in 18th. century Newfoundland and sometimes they were the cause of rivalry that ended in violence between their would-be suitors. However, more often than not the women were the victims.

Ann Stephens and the Trepassey Men:

One of the first recorded cases involving trouble over a girl came from the complaint of John Rose, a planter at Trepassey. He complained to the Governor that on March 3, 1751, Matthew Kennedy, Robert Wheeler, James Ward and John Maher entered his house by breaking down the door. They then beat his servants, Patrick and Simeon Fennessey and James Stafford "to the effusion of their blood." An investigation into the complaint indicated that Ann Stephens also of Trepassey had been the cause of the trouble. She had been in the company of the five men when they entered Rose's house. The governor took a dim view of these activities and ordered each of the five men involved to receive 39 lashes. He also ordered Ann Stephens to have someone act as security for her good behaviour or she too would feel the lash.[2]

---

1   *Colonial Letterbook*, Volume 1, July, 1750.
2   *Ibid.*

The Case of John Stripling's Lamb:

On the 12th of September, 1759, a soldier at the fort in St. John's named William Kitchon appeared in court charged with killing and eating a lamb, the property of Mr. John Stripling. Two Irish women, Margaret Power and Catherine Shea (alias Crimmings) who lived in the same house as Kitchon were also charged with having knowledge of the crime, and helping to conceal part of the lamb carcass. William Kitchon pleaded guilty to killing the lamb. Mary Power and Alice Shea pleaded not guilty to having any part in the affair. John Earles, the constable, was the only one to give evidence. He testified as follows:

> That the said John Earles by virtue of a search warrant from Michael Gill Esq. went to May Aldrige's house to search for a lamb stolen from John Stripling and found in the said house William Kitchon also Margaret Power and Catherine Shea alias Crimming. The said Kitchon offered to show him the said deponent all over the said house, but in the meantime the said Kitchon went and took down part of the said lamb which was put away concealed up over the bed where the said Margaret Power lay wrapped up in pease stalks and endeavoured to get away to conceal the same. Deponent followed him and struck up his heels and took it from him., then, this Kitchon when he found that he was apprehended acknowledged himself guilty of killing the lamb, but the said deponent never heard the said Kitchon say that the said Margaret Power and Katherine Shea alias Crimming was accessories to the theft and further this deponent sayaeth not.

There was no other evidence presented and without leaving the room the jury found the two Irish women not guilty through lack of evidence. William Kitchon stood guilty by his own confession. Power and Shea were dismissed from court and Kitchon was sentenced to be burnt on the hand with the letter "R."[1]

Justice for the Irish on Fogo Island:

At Tilting Harbour, on Fogo Island in 1759 an Irish resident, Patrick Murphy, who was obviously a planter, went in debt to the tune of 102 pounds, 1 shilling and 3 pence to William Keene, his supplier. Murphy was ordered to pay the bill.

The same year, another Irishman, Francis Fleming of Tilting, complained that his master William Chalk had paid him his wages in fish instead of bills of exchange and then taken back the fish. The governor ordered Chalk to pay Fleming 16 pounds less 3 pounds 10 shillings, which was Fleming's account with Chalk.

In 1762 William Sullivan, an Irish servant at Tilting, presented a petition to the governor that he had served John Power at Tilting from September 21, 1761 to August 1, 1762 at which time he was forced to leave Power for want of provisions. Sullivan had offered to discount for the time lost but Power refused and also refused to honour a note of hand for 3 pounds, 5 shillings and 8 pence. The governor did not make an immediate decision on this case but ordered the local Justice of the Peace to investigate the complaint.[2]

Trouble At Trinity:

In 1759, David Lacey of Trinity petitioned the governor that he had supplied John Doyle and his brother, both of Trinity, with provisions to the amount of 5 pounds sterling, which John Doyle refused to pay when the fishing voyage was finished. The governor settled the matter by ordering William Reeves, Doyle's master to stop this money from his wages and pay it to David Lacey.

---

1 *Colonial Letterbook*, September, 1759
2 *Colonial Letterbook*, Volume 11, 1762

Another complaint from Trinity in 1759 came from Matthew Hennessey. He had been a servant to Michael Tracey and John Welsh and claimed he had been attacked and abused by his masters. He said that without any provocation, Michael Tracey came behind him when he was at work and beat him most inhumanely. Then, adding insult to injury, Tracey stripped him of his clothes and took his shipping papers. He begged Tracey to return his shipping papers, but Tracey would neither give him back his shipping papers nor take him back as a servant. The governor ordered Tracey and Welsh to pay Hennessey for the fishing season.

In 1762, John Lemnon, a Trinity merchant fled for fear of a French attack on the community. When he returned to Trinity he refused to pay the wages due his Irish servants according to an agreement signed in the spring of 1762. The case came to the attention of the governor who ordered Lemnon to pay the following amounts:

Name	Amount due
Philip Murphy	23 pounds
John Connoll	10 "
Pat Coffee	10 "
William Keefe	10 "
Edward Walsh	10 "

At the same court Pat Whelan of Trinity sued Pat Ducey for non payment of wages and again the governor ruled in his favour.

Non Payment of Fishing Wages at Ochre Pit Cove, 1762:

At Ochre Pit Cove, Conception Bay in 1762, an Irish servant, John Keating, petitioned the governor against his master for non-payment of wages. Again the governor supported the fisherman against his master and ordered the wages paid.

The Irish in Harbour Main:

There was an interesting case of non payment of wages at Harbour Main in 1762. Here a master in poor circumstances, Robert Finn, offered Nicholas Welsh 13 pounds for his summer wages or a boat with masts and oars, if the fishery miscarried, and 5 pounds 14 shillings in "truck" for his winter wages. Finn had neither paid the wages nor given the boat at the end of the voyage. Welsh brought his case to the governor who ordered Finn to pay the wages due.

Confirmation of an Irish Woman's Right to hold Property:

In 1765, Mary McDonald, an Irish woman living in Harbour Main, petitioned the governor to confirm her ownership of a fish room in that community. The governor did not give her outright possession, but ruled that she could hold the fish room in question until someone with a better claim than she came forward with proof of a better title. He further added that no one was to turn her from the room she now occupied.

Illegal Seizure of Goods at St. Mary's:

At the harbour of St. Mary's, an Irish planter, John Ryan, was accused by Thomas Townshend of seizing property from him while the French were in control of St. John's in 1762. The governor ordered the Fishing Admiral at St. Mary's to investigate the matter and help Townshend get his property back.

The next year William O'Brien of St. Mary's was also accused of taking advantage of the French occupation to seize both wet and dry fish from Thomas Keates of the same place. It was also charged that O'Brien had taken salmon and bread that Keates had stored at Salmonier without any account to Keates, with the exception of four tierces of salmon he had given to Keates servant, Maurice Ahern. The governor ordered the Fishing Admiral of St. Mary's to inquire into the complaint and O'Brien was ordered to pay Keates for the property taken.

Accusation of the Murder of An Irishman at Forteau.

In 1766 the first report of an Irish presence on the Labrador coast came with the report of the murder of an Irishman named Nugent at Forteau. Nugent was reported to have been barbarously murdered by the crew members of a fishing ship at Forteau. The report to the governor on this matter suggested that the same crew had murdered another man at the Isle de Bois during the same summer. An investigation into the affair showed that the crews of both ships had been British with the exception of Nugent and a man named Dillon. The crews involved were arrested and brought to trial at St. John's

Justice for an Irish Servant at Petty Harbour:

At Petty Harbour In 1767, Andre Churchwood, a planter, refused to pay Patrick Power, his Irish servant, his wages of 7 pounds 10 shillings and provide a passage back to Ireland. Power appealed to the governor who examined his shipping papers and Churchwood was ordered to pay the debt or appear at court in St. John's to explain his actions. Churchwood paid up.[1]

A Fishery Scam at Harbour Grace:

In 1767 Felix McCarthy, an Irish merchant at Harbour Grace, was caught out in a scheme to avoid paying the wages of fishing servants by hiring an insolvent debtor, Thomas English, as a fishing master and supplying him with a craft and provisions for the fishery. At the end of the season the fish went to McCarthy for past debts and the insolvent master was unable to pay his crew. The crew petitioned the governor and he, seeing through the scheme, ordered McCarthy to pay the men's wages and their passage home to Ireland. The governor also ordered that if McCarthy or his agent did not provide

1 *Colonial Lettrbook*, 1759, p.27.

the men's passage home, then the five men were to quarter themselves on McCarthy or his agent for the winter, and McCarthy was to see that the men had sufficient food. The men involved were:

John Fowler	William Nugent
Matt Kennedy	Maurice Walsh
John Mead	Morgan Sherridan

A Scheme to Defraud the Irish servants at Greenspond:

There were Irishmen serving in the fishery at Greenspond by 1767, and James Hayward, a merchant of the community, invoked the same scheme as Felix McCarthy of Harbour Grace to avoid paying his servants. He hired an insolvent debtor named Pat Ducey as a master and supplied him with a craft and provisions for the fishing voyage. Ducey delivered the fish to Hayward who took most of it for supplying Ducey. Ducey was then unable to pay his crew. Again, the governor intervened and ordered Hayward to pay the 13 crew members who were:

Jermiah Daniel	Pat Ducey	John Carey
Ed. Pendergrass	Maurice Mulchey	Richard Maugher
Tom Kearich	John Higgins	William Calimon
Pat Bryan	Matt Power	John Daniel
Lawrence Bryan		

Few Irish Involved in Major Crimes:

The number of Irish appearing in court for violent crimes was very small. The majority of Irish servants lived peaceably with their neighbours, and their fights, often the result of the consumption of too much liquor, were usually among themselves. Except when the governor or naval officer intervened, the Irish were at the mercy of their masters, being aliens in race and religion to those in power. Yet it should be pointed out to the everlasting credit of these all-powerful naval governors, that when cases of injustice to the Irish regarding their rightful wages and other matters came to the governor's attention, his decisions were usually in favour of the Irish servant. The statement made by Rodney to the magistrates of Harbour Grace in 1749 would also apply to most of his successors. Even while the governors were framing rules and regulations to limit their number, the Irish were still entitled to justice in matters of ill treatment and in obtaining their rightful wages.

Chapter Three

The Quidi Vidi Murder and Its Consequences

Until 1755, the Irish population of Newfoundland suffered under no special restrictions despite the fears expressed by various naval officers and governors. However, on September 9th, 1754, an event took place that was to see a rigid enforcement of the penal laws and the active persecution of the Irish Roman Catholics in Newfoundland. As well, over the next two decades a number of laws were passed to hamper and restrict their staying in the island.

The event was the robbery of the house of William Keene Sr., an important merchant and one of the Justices of the Peace for St. John's. In the execution of the robbery on the night of September 9th., 1754, William Keene was wounded and died on September 29th.

The robbery of Keene's house in Quidi Vidi was organized by Eleanor Power, a young Irish woman, who lived at Blackhead in Freshwater Bay near St. John's. Eleanor had come out from Ireland as a servant girl to serve in Keene's house. When her time of employment was finished she married Robert Power, a fisherman who resided in Blackhead. Eleanor knew that Keene kept a chest of gold in his house to finance his business and especially for buying ships taken as war prizes. In her plan to rob Keene's house in the summer of 1754, she enlisted the help of her husband and eight other Irishmen, three of them soldiers stationed at St. John's. One of them was Edmund McGuire, who was waiting to be tried for assaulting William Murphy, the assistant to Constable John Worth. They carefully carried out their plan, and thought they had had killed Keene, but he lived long enough to identify Eleanor as one of the robbers and they were all taken. One of their number, Nicholas Tobin, turned king's evidence and the fate of the others was sealed. His evidence was very alarming to the authorities and English merchants for it showed the casualness with which the group planned the murder and the impunity with which they put the plan into action.

According to Tobin's evidence, around the end of August he was returning to the fort from Blackhead in a skiff with Robert Power, Eleanor Power, Matthew Halleran, Edmund McGuire, Paul McDonald and Lawrence Lambly. On the way in Eleanor Power asked him if he knew where they were going? He replied that he did not. Then, Eleanor swore him to secrecy on a prayer book and told him they were on their way to rob Keene's house of a chest of gold. At this point Lawrence Lambly invited him to join with them and he agreed. They landed at the King's wharf where they were joined by another soldier named Hawkins and went to Keene's summerhouse. After some time they were joined by John Moody and John Munshall who also lived in Blackhead. The band of robbers swore to be true to each other and sealed their oath by kissing Eleanor's prayer book.

At midnight, Halleran, McGuire and Lambly went out to see if the coast was clear. They returned quickly to say that there were a lot of people splitting fish in the fish stages near Keene's house. As a result they decided it would be too risky to carry out the robbery that night and returned to their homes at the fort and Blackhead to wait a more favourable opportunity.

A few days later the band of robbers assembled again. This time the people from Blackhead walked overland to St. John's and met the soldiers at Keene's summerhouse. They had two muskets, two bayonets which the soldiers provided, and Halleran had the top of a scythe blade. This time Halleran was sent to spy out the land. He came back to say that Keene's son, William Junior, had just landed at his father's wharf and there would be too many in the house to carry out the robbery. Again they had to return home empty handed, but agreed to make one last attempt to carry out their plan.

On the morning of September 9, 1754, Tobin went to Blackhead to Robert Power's house and it was agreed that they would make another attempt to rob Keene's house that night. Tobin came back to St. John's and alerted the soldiers involved in the plot. At ten o'clock they began to arrive at Keene's summerhouse and by midnight all hands had arrived. They then proceeded to put their plan into action.

Tobin was appointed watchman near Mr. Squarry's room next to Keene's house. He was given one of the muskets and told to fire on anyone who might seek to examine him too closely. Robert Power was stationed at the corner of Ed Wheatland's house with the other musket and orders similar to those of Tobin. Denis Hawkins also stood guard to warn those who went inside if any one came near. Eleanor Power—dressed in men's clothing—Ed McGuire, Matthew Halleran, Lawrence Lambly, John Moody and John Munshall forced the lock on the door and entered Keen's house. Paul McDonald was placed as guard at the door.

The party that entered the house came out bringing a case that Eleanor claimed contained the gold. Lambly and Halleran also took a number of silver spoons that they found. They then went to the summerhouse to divide their spoils. McGuire broke open the case and to the utter disappointment of the robbers it contained French wines and brandy instead of gold. Tobin described what happened next:

> Then Eleanor Power and Lawrence Lambly both went from us. This deponent further saith that on being disappointed he and Denis Hawkins were for going from the others, but John Munshall took hold of him and said we should all go to Mr. Keen's a second time, and Ed McGuire said that he would shoot any that went from them, and that he was sorry he had not shot the woman (Eleanor). John Munshall told this deponent to take one of the bottles out of the case and drink a dram. This deponent further saith Edmund McGuire said that he would be revenged upon Mr. Keen for something that had passed between them—Keen had ordered McGuire whipped for being drunk and disorderly some months previously—and the said Ed McGuire and Matthew Halleran said that if they could not get the money and Mr. Keen would not tell them where the money was they would punish him. Then, we all except Eleanor Power and Lawrence Lambly went down a second time to Mr. Keene's house. Denis Hawkins and this deponent were placed at Edward Whealand's door, each with a gun in our hands to keep Edward Whealand in his house that he might not come out and make a noise. Robert Power stood in the main path with a gun in his hand and Paul McDonald stood at Mr. Keene's kitchen door. Edmund Mcguire, John Moody, John Munshall and Matthew Halleran entered the house, and this deponent further saith that Matthew Halleran told him that he and Edmund McGuire went from the kitchen up the stairs into Mr. Keene's room where they found him in bed, and that he Halleran took out a box from under the bed and that Mr. Keene waked upon which Edmund McGuire put the quilt over Mr. Keene's head. Mr. Keene then rose up in his bed and with his hands put out the candle which the said Mcguire had in his hands and caught hold of Halleran by the leg and cried out "Murder" and that said Halleran told him he struck Mr. Keene twice with the scythe which the said Halleran had in his hand and

that he had done his business and he could not recover. And this deponent further saith that Edmund McGuire told him that he gave Mr. Keene a stroke with the butt end of a musket and that he had some of Mr. Keene's blood on his hands, and that the said McGuire took a pair of knee buckles and one single buckle and this deponent further saith that Robert Power say'd when they were disappointed the first time of getting Mr. Keene's money that the best way was to go down the second time and if Mr. Keene would not show them where his money was they should punish him in a way that he would not recover. This deponent saith that he never saw John Moody at anytime at their meetings before that the robbery and murder was committed and further saith not.[1]

Following Tobin's testimony, two St. John's surgeons, Thomas Allan and John Burton who had attended Mr. Keene after the attack, gave evidence. They testified that Keene had died as a direct result of the wounds inflicted on his body on the night of September 9th.

Edmund McGuire testified he had nothing to say in his own defence—but declared that only he and Halleran had been in the room when Mr. Keene had been wounded; he carried a gun and Halleran had a piece of an old scythe with a sharp point. Halleran had struck Keene with the scythe top and he had given Keene a blow in the breast with the gun. He also identified all the members of the gang and said Robert Power had wanted to murder Keene from the first.

Robert Power and Eleanor Power, his wife, testified next and said they had nothing to say in their own defence, but they were not guilty of murder. John Moody said he had been persuaded by McGuire to go on the robbery on the night of September 9 and he had been part of the other two robbery attempts. He begged the court "not to take away my life."

1 *Colonial Letterbook*, Volume 1, October 1754

John Munshall said he too had been recruited by McGuire for the robbery but had taken no part in the murder. He had been guarding the servant's door to the kitchen and Edmund McGuire had come downstairs all covered in blood. He also said that Robert Power had first said they should kill Mr. Keene, but then said he would not go in the house if they meant to kill him. He had heard that it was Halleran who had cut Mr. Keene. The others pleaded in a similar way. They did not deny being at the house with the intention of robbing it, but excused themselves from being actually involved in the murder, and begged that the court would spare their lives.

The Death Sentence:

Then the charge was given to the jury. They retired for half an hour and returned with a verdict of guilty for all charged on two counts of felony and murder. The prisoners were then asked again if there was any reason sentence should not be passed on them, and they replied there was not and threw themselves on the mercy of the court. Sentence was then passed:

> That you Edmund McGuire, Matthew Halleran, Robert Power, Eleanor Power, Lawrence Lambly Paul McDonald, John Moody, John Munshall and Denis Hawkins, be sent back to the place from whence you came and from thence to the place of execution and there be hanged by the neck until you are dead, dead, dead, and the Lord have mercy on your soul.
>
> And that Edmund McGuire and Matthew Halleran after being dead and taken down are to be hanged in chains in some public place when and where the Governor shall be pleased to appoint.[1]

---

1 *Colonial Letterbook*, Volume 1, Keene Murder Trial.

On October 8, Governor Bonfoy sent the following directive to William Thomas, the Sheriff of Newfoundland:

> You are hereby requird and directed to immediately on
> receipt hereof to cause a Gibbet to be erected capable of
> containing two men in chains. The officer that brings you
> this will inform you the place where. And for so doing this
> shall be your sufficient authority.[1]

On October 10, 1754, Edmund McGuire and Matthew
Halleran were hanged and then their bodies were taken
down and hung in chains on Gibbet Hill. The following day,
October 11th, Eleanor Power and her husband Robert were
hanged together at noon on Keene's wharf. Their bodies
were taken down and buried near the place of execution.
Eleanor Power thus became the first woman to be executed
in Newfoundland, and when Newfoundland joined Canada
in 1949, this became the first execution of a woman in
Canada.

The other prisoners were then ordered confined to the
"brig" at the fort until His Majesty's pleasure should be
known concerning them. According to testimony given by
John Kennedy the following year, Lambly was also executed.
In 1757 the other prisoners received a Royal Pardon, but
were ordered transported out of the Island of Newfoundland.

However, the affair did not end here. The following
summer, William Keene Jr. obtained a deposition from a
James Kennedy who was fishing for him at Greenspond.
Kennedy admitted that in March of 1754 he had met
Lawrence Lambly and Matthew Halleran while coming from
the River of St. John's and they had invited him to go with
them to rob Mr. Keene's house which, they said, Robert
Poor's wife said contained a great quantity of money. He

1 *Letterbook* Volume 1.

refused and they charged him not to tell anyone about the robbery. He promised to say nothing and told no one about the conversation. This testimony was alarming to the English planters for it showed that although other Irish servants had known of the plot to rob Keene's house, they had neither warned the authorities nor the threatened person of the plot against him.

On the 15th. of September, 1755, Kennedy appeared at a court of Oyer and Terminer and gave the following evidence on the Keene's affair:

> The following declaration taken at the Court House 15th September 1755. The witness James Kennedy further confesses that some time before Lawrence Lambly and Matthew Halleran asked him to go with them to rob Mr. Keene's house, Lawrence Kavanaugh met him in the path and told him he kept bad company and mentioned Matthew Halleran and Lawrence Lambly, and that Halleran and Lambly said they would go about Easter and rob Mr. Keene's house, if the said Kennedy would go along with them who answered that he never would and that he never kept company with the two men afterwards, but the latter part of May went to Witless Bay and took service with John Carey and did not return to the place until after the said Halleran and Lambly were executed.[1]

The court took a dim view of Kennedy's silence and he was found guilty of being an accomplice to the crime and sentenced to be burnt on the right hand with the letter "R" and then transported out of Newfoundland. This was the final charge in the Keene murder. However, the repercussions from that murder were to affect the general Irish population of Newfoundland for decades to come.

-----

1 *Colonial Letterbook*, September 1755.

Religious Persecution in Conception Bay:

What was most disturbing to the Newfoundland authorities about the Keene murder was the revelation that other Irishmen knew of the plans to rob Keene's house, but would not betray their fellow countrymen by alerting the victim. As well, Tobin in his evidence at the Keene trial had revealed that McGuire had wished to be revenged on Keene for ordering him confined to the fort and transported out of Newfoundland for assaulting the constable and Andrew Murphy his assistant the previous February. While waiting transportation, McGuire had helped plan and carry out the Keene robbery and murder. It was clear to the governor and magistrates that something would have to be done to check the rapid growth of the Irish population in Newfoundland.

Mass celebrated at Harbour Grace:

The first active religious persecution of the Newfoundland Irish was set in motion in August, 1755, when Governor Dorrill wrote to George Garland, the Harbour Grace magistrate, concerning a Roman Catholic priest who had been reported in the area.

> Whereas I am informed that a Roman Catholic priest is at this time at Harbour Grace, and that he publicly read mass which is contrary to law, and against the peace of our sovereign lord the king. You are hereby required and directed on the receipt of this to cause the said priest to be taken into custody and sent round to this place (St. John's) and in this you are not to fail.[1]

Magistrate Garland replied to Governor Dorrill on August 22, 1755:

---

1 Prowse,p. 294

Hr. Grace
August 22, 1755
Excellent Sir:
   As there is little prospect of catching more fish this
season, the scheme of the fishery shall soon be filled out
and sent you, as concerning the Roman Priest of whom you
were informed that he read public mass in Hr. Grace, 'twas
misrepresented to you, 'twas at a place called Caplin Cove
somewhat below the Hr., for he if he read mass in the Hr.,
I should have known and would have secured him. After he
was informed I had intelligence of him, he immediately left
the place and I was yesterday informed he was gone to
Harbour Main.
Sir
Your most obedient servant
George Garland[1]

Governor Dorrill immediately sent troops from the fort at
St. John's to Harbour Main to catch the priest. They were not
successful and an oral tradition in the community says the
priest was hidden in a cellar and after dark spirited away to
the neighbouring community of Conception Harbour—then
called Cat's Cove—and then to communities further down
the shore. However, an informer at Harbour Main revealed
the names of the persons who had attended a mass said at
Harbour Main by the itinerant priest.

   The priest was never taken, but all the persons who
attended mass in the different Conception Bay communities
were punished. The first trial for those accused of attending
mass was held at Harbour Grace on September 15, 1755. The
judge was Thomas Burnell Esq., Deputy Surrogate to Governor Dorrill. The evidence showed that Governor Dorrill's
information had been correct. Despite Mr. Garland's denial,
mass had been said at Harbour Grace.

---

1 *Colonial LetterBook* Volume 11, September, 1755.

Whereas it has been represented to me at court held this day at Harbour Grace, at which you George and Charles Garland were present at which time it did appear that public mass was celebrated according to the Church of Rome in one of Mr. Stretche's storehouses on Sunday, July 26, 1755, although it appears he was not in the harbour that day, but most of men and women servants was there and the door not being locked to prevent any such congregation to assemble for which neglect we think proper to fine him the sum of ten pounds sterling and the said storehouse to be burnt down to the ground. Which fine is to be made use of towards defraying the expenses the governor shall be at in sending his deputy in the Northern Circuit of the island.

I do hereby require and direct you George and Charles Garland H. M. Justices of the Peace to see the said sentence put into execution by tomorrow morning by eleven o'clock, 16th September, 1755. Given under my hand at Harbour Grace.

T. Burnett.[1]

Mass Celebrated at Musketa Cove:

At the same court sitting at Harbour Grace it was declared that as mass had been said in Darby Crawley's house in Musketa Cove, it was proper that the said house be burnt to the ground.

Mass celebrated at Harbour Main:

On September 20, the court moved to Harbour Main and the full force of the law was felt by Michael Katen (Keating) for permitting the priest to say mass in his fish store and also for attending the mass in person. He pleaded guilty to both charges and was fined fifty pounds. The Surrogate also ordered that Katen's fishstore should be burnt to the ground

---

1 *Ibid*

and that he must sell all his possessions and quit the harbour before November 25, 1755.

At the same court Michael Landrigan was fined twenty pounds, and had his house and stage burnt. Also fined with Landrigan were Darby Costley, Robert Finn, Michael Mooring and Robert McDonald. Their fines varied from ten pounds to two pounds each and they were ordered to quit the harbour at the same time as Katen.

On September 21, the court again sat at Harbour Main and, acting on information received, charged another group of Harbour Main men with attending mass.

At a court held at Harbour Main, September 20, 1755, at which you Charles Garland was present, one of his Majesty's Justices of the Peace, at which time did appear before us, Martin Donnelly, John Sennot, John Devereaux, Robert Tobin, John Gusho, William Welsh, Tom Ryan, Mick Hanlon, William Murphy, Michael Hannigan, Thomas Connolly, George McDonald, John Rossena, Tom Hoiden, John Welsh, John Clancy, Robert Breman, all of which are Roman Catholic and servants to Michael Katen and did all join in celebrating public mass in his fish store for which we think proper to fine viz: M. Donnelly 1 pound, John Sennott 2 pounds, Devereaux 2 pounds, Tobin 1 pound, Wm. Welsh, Ryan and Hanlon 2 pounds each, Wm Murphy 3 pounds, Connolly 1 pound, McDonald 2 pounds, Hoiden 3 pounds, J. Welsh 3 pounds, Clancy 3 pounds, which fines the above persons do pay to Michael Katen or order towards making good the damages he received by demolishing his fish room.

To Michael Katen, Harbour Main, given under my hand at Harbour Grace 20th., of September 1755.[1]

---

1   Ibid

The magistrate also ordered that the fines from Michael Katen and the Harbour Main men convicted in the first case should go towards the building of gaol at Harbour Main. This goal would be for securing any vagabonds that should desert from any part of the island. Pedley says that a warship which was at Holyrood came to Harbour Main and hauled Katen's store out in the harbour where it was burnt.[1]

Mass celebrated at Carbonear:

The court cases against those attending mass in various Conception Bay communities continued. On September 25, 1755, a court was held at Carbonear:

> Whereas at a court held at Carbonear the 25th of September at which you Mullins and Garland were present at which time it did appear that public mass was celebrated according to the Church of Rome in William Pike's house which was then inhabited by Morthaugh McGuire and Morgan Hogan, neither of them appearing to answer the charges laid against them, we think proper to fine McGuire 20 pounds and Hogan 15 pounds and they to quit this place and this island before October 10th ensuing, and the said house to be demolished and said fines after paying 10 pounds for court fees the remainder to go towards paying for the damages to the house.[2]

At the same court, Sept Crawley of Carbonear was also convicted of allowing mass to be said in his house, he was fined and his house ordered demolished. It must have been cold comfort to William Pike that the remainder of the thirty-five pounds levied against McGuire and Hogan were to be his. As they had not appeared in court it was certain they had fled the area or they would have been arrested and

---

1 Howley, p.173
2 Ibid

hauled into court. The court cases continued and the Kennedy's of Crocker's Cove were next charged with not only attending mass, but with getting married during the celebration.

> Whereas at a court held at Crocker's Cove, September 25, 1755, at which you R. Mullins and Thomas Garland were present at which time it did appear before us that public mass was read in Terrence Kennedy's house and the said Kennedy and his wife married by the priest which does appear in the confession of Mary Kennedy, his wife.
>
> We therefore think proper to fine said Kennedy the sum of 10 pounds sterling money for payment of court fees and to burn his house down to the ground and that he quit this place and likewise this island of Newfoundland on or before October ensuing. Given under my hand at Crocker's Cove Sept. 25, 1755. T. Burnett

However, an informer was at work again and the names of the persons who attended the mass in Terrence Kennedy's house were given to the Justice of the Peace. Again it was the owner of the house who profited from the fines levied:

> Whereas at a court held at Carbonear September 25th., at which R. Mullins and C. Garland were present at which time it appeared that J. Whelan, Nick Leoline, Ed. O'Brien, Darby Connors, Wm. Kennedy, Wm. Hennessey, John Power, Mick Hickey, Pat Whelan and Nick Scanline, all which are servants to Terence Kennedy and were at mass with him for which we think proper to fine them John Whelan 3 pounds, Nick Leoline 2 pounds, Ed O'Brien 2 pounds, Darby Connors 2 pounds, Wm. Hennessey 2 pounds, Pat Whelan 1 pound, Wm. Kennedy 1 pound 10 shillings, Mick Hickey 1 pound 10 shillings, john Power 1 pound 10 shillings, the whole sum amounting to 18 pounds 10 shillings which fines are to go to Terrence Kennedy towards defraying the damages sustained in

burning his house. Given at Carbonear, September 25, 1755.

T. Burnett[1]

The final court case in the religious persecutions of the Irish Roman Catholics in Conception Bay ended on September 26 when John Kennedy, of Crocker's Cove was tried in absentia at Harbour Grace. He was sentenced to pay a fine of six pounds sterling for court fees and to leave Newfoundland before the 10th of October, 1755.

However, the itinerant priests who came to minister to the Irish Roman Catholic fishermen and settlers continued to be hunted by the authorities. At Witless Bay one priest was actually in a fishing boat disguised as a fisherman when soldiers searched it for a reported Roman Catholic priest. Another priest had a narrow escape at Toad's Cove (Tor's Cove) and had to be hidden in a cellar. There is also a "Midnight Rock" at Renews where mass was said secretly and the Rosary recited in the days of persecution.[2]

Along with ordering an active religious persecution of the Irish in Newfoundland, Governor Dorrill drafted regulations to reduce the Irish population and make it more difficult for new arrivals to stay in the Island. On September 22, 1755, he issued the first restrictions on Irish Roman Catholics coming to Newfoundland:

> Whereas a great number of Irish Roman Catholics are annually brought over here, a great part of which have but small wages, so that after paying their passage to this place and the charges of clothing etc. during the fish season, their whole wages are spent and they have not the where-withal to pay their passage home, or purchase provisions for the winter, by which means they not only become

---

1   Ibid p. 261
2   Howley p. 181

chargeable to this place, but many robberies and felonies are committed by them to the great loss and terror of His Majesty's Liege subjects in this island.

This is therefore to warn and give notice to all masters of ships or vessels which bring passengers to this island that after the fishing season they carry from hence the whole number and same passengers they bring here except such as man have my order to remain in this island, and hereafter they are not to fail, as they will be proceeded against with the greatest severity the law in such cases will permit. Given under my hand
at St. John's, Sept. 22, 1755
Governor Dorrill[1]

Petition of the Principal Traders of Harbour Grace:

Encouraged by the official anti-Irish sentiments the people of Harbour Grace sent a petition to the governor protesting the establishment of a small Irish community at Riverhead, Harbour Grace. The petition read:

The Humble Petition of the Principal Traders and inhabitants of Harbour Grace:
Sheweth:
That your petitioners have for some time past been greatly injured by loosing their cattle, sheep etc., which they suspect have been stolen by persons which inhabit the same place but rendezvousing in several little houses, lately erected in the upper end of the said Harbour. That the persons who dwell in the said hutts or houses are people of loose and bad character harbouring number of persons which from their not entering service make them suspect of being guilty of said crime.
Signed:

| Nicholas Tynt | Stephen Wittle | Wm. Dawson |
| Philip Payne | Nick Juer | Francis Shepherd |

---

1 Ibid.

Ed. Coombs	Tom Parsons	Robert Andrews
M. Streetch	Henry Wethers	John Martin
Mary Martin	Ed. Snow	Wm. Martin[1]

This petition was accepted by the governor but no action was taken against the Riverhead community.

Christian Brothers Fourth Reader

Mass being celebrated at a Mass Rock, similar to the one performed at Renews

1 *Colonial Letterbook*, volume 11

Harbour Main, where religious persecution took place in 1755

Chapter Four

The Expansion of the Irish Population in Newfoundland

Increased Irish Immigration:

Despite the religious persecution of the Irish following the Keene murder, the Irish population in Newfoundland continued to expand with a flow of Irish workers brought over by unscrupulous fishing captains. In fact, on October 28, 1757, Governor Edwards in a letter to the Board of Trade complained of the great number of Irish coming to Newfoundland:

> It having being a custom for some time past for fishing ships not to bring with them from England their complete number of green-men, and abreech of the laudable custom of allowing shares of what they make in a fishing voyage, instead of wages, they have had recourse to getting over a number of Irishmen, who being generally Roman Catholics, they use them as they think proper, and seldom pay them any wages, by which many of them are left on the Island, to the great terror and distress of the Inhabitants.[1]

---

1   Innis Harold, *The Cod Fishery*, Revised Edition, p. 153.

In 1766, Reverend Edward Langman, the Church of England priest at St. John's reported that:

> There was a greater number of poor Irish men brought here (Newfoundland) this spring from Waterford than has been known in one year before, for 14 years past.

Joseph Banks Account of the Newfoundland Irish in 1766

In the fall of 1766, famous British scientist Joseph Banks visited St. John's and wrote that one could see and smell "The remains of the Irish men's chowder who you see making it, skinning and gutting fish in every Corner." He went on to record that during and after the French attack and capture of St. John's in May of 1762, 700 Irishmen immediately went into the service of the French. He said that in 1765-66 the number of houses in St. John's was 300 and the permanent population was 1100 made up of 750 men, and 350 women and children. That out of this winter population in St. John's the Irish more than doubled the English. In other areas the Irish outnumbered the English ten to one. Of the total population of the Island 1/18 was deemed to be Irish Roman Catholics and untrustworthy.[1]

Irish Presence in Many Outport Communities

From the Court cases in the Governor's Letterbook we can see that after 1750, the Irish had indeed settled in many of the communities scattered around the Newfoundland coastline.

First Irish Settler On Bell Island:

In 1765 the first mention of an Irish inhabitant appears in the records. For in that year it was reported that James O'Neil had cleared land and built a house on Bell Island.

---

1 *Joseph Banks in Newfoundland and Labrador*, 1766. Ed. by A.M. Lysaght, p.151.

Illegal Occupation of a Fish Room at Tilting:

In 1767, the Governor was informed that two Irishmen had illegaly taken possession of a fishing room at Tilting. He promptly issued the following edict:

> Whereas it hath been reported to me that Cornelius Lene-han and Maurice Power hold and possess a fishing room at Tilting Harbour, with sundry fishing works thereon, not erected by themselves, nor at their expense, that the said two men, Lenehan and Power, are not qualified to hold a fishing room according to the Act of the 11th of William 111 which required that every fifth man shall be a new or "Greenman" from Britain yearly, besides the coast to the northward of Bonavista being held by the King's orders, declared all ships rooms for concurrent fishery of English and French ships. I thereby authorize any British fishing ship qualified as such with the usual fishing certificate.[1]

The Merry Widow of Fogo:

In 1771 at Fogo Mrs. Mary Bond, the widow of the late Joseph Bond, a bye-boat keeper of that place, kicked up her heels a bit. She annoyed the Fishing Admiral and several other of the principal citizens so much that they complained of her conduct to the Governor and asked that she be deported back to Ireland. The governor, however, gave her one more chance to amend her ways. He ordered the Fishing Admiral at Fogo to admonish Mary, to tell her to stop her disorderly conduct and if she did not obey, the Fishing Admiral was to put her on the first ship bound for Ireland.[2]

Irish Smugglers In Fortune and Placentia Bays:

On July 4, 1765, the governor issued a deportation order for Bryant Flaherty, an Irish planter of Long Harbour, Fortune

---

1 *Colonial Letterbook*, 1767
2 *Colonial Letterbook*, 1770

Bay. He had been caught trading with the French at St. Pierre and bringing goods from St. Pierre to Long Harbour. His property was sold off and he was ordered to leave the island.

The following year Thomas Speering of St. Lawrence was also convicted of smuggling . His goods were also ordered sold and he was deported with his family to England.

The Irish at Bonavista:

In 1771, the magistrate at Bonavista reported that an Irishman had defied the law and put a claim on a fishing room in Bonavista and without leave or license intended to build a stage on the site.

The governor was outraged and wrote to the magistrate at Bonavista:

> Whereas you have represented to me that an Irish Papist, a servant, a man without wife or family has put up posts on a fishing room within your district with an intent to build a stage and flake thereon for possession of same as his RIGHT OF PROPERTY, which is contrary to the Act of William 111.
>
> I do hereby authorize you to immediately cause the mark posts above mentioned to be taken down and warn the person offending not to presume to mark out any other fishing room again as his property or he will answer to the contrary.[1]

Settlement of Irish Papists Near Bonavista:

In 1774, the Bonavista magistrate was very upset when he was informed that a group of Irish Papists had settled at Bird Island Cove, near Bonavista and here offered in the words of Magistrate William Keene, *"assistance when they flee from the law to all evil persons, where stolen goods have been conveyed and which has become a pest to society."* The

---

1 Ibid

governor ordered the magistrates to use every legal means to dislodge them and send tham back to Ireland.

The Obstreperous Irishman of St. Juliens:

Sometime before the summer of 1763, an Irishman named John Dunien in defiance of the law established a fishing room at St. Juliens on the "Treaty Coast." In the summer of 1763, a French fishing captain arrived at St. Juliens and tried to take possession of Dunien's room under the Fishing Admiral's right to first choice of fishing rooms in a community. Dunien refused to give up his fishing room without a fight, and successfully repulsed the French Captain's attempt to take possession of his property. In fact as the old records report, "he became so obstreperous in his altercations with the French" that they appealed to Governor Palliser in St. John's. Palliser immediately ordered Dunien seized and deported, and added that he was to be whipped if he attempted to return to St. Juliens. Dunien however made his escape before the English authorities could take him, and most likely settled in some other uninhabited cove outside the French jurisdiction.

Oderin:

At Oderin in Placentia Bay, there was court work in 1762 over a plantation known as the "Blue Beach." The plantation in question was claimed by the mother of Jack Crawley Richards. Another resident of Oderin, John Roach, seized the "Blue Beach," but the governor ordered it returned to Mrs Richards whom he declared was the rightful owner.

Passage to Harbour Grace:

On April 1, 1776, the following advertisment for fishermen for Newfoundland appeared in an Irish newspaper named the

Hibernian Chronicle:
For Harbour Grace Newfoundland
The *Hannah & Lydia* of Cork John Collins will be ready to
sail the 10th, of April. For passage apply to said master at
cove. Fishermen, shoreman and youngsters all wanted.
March 23, 1776[1]

Irish On The Southern Shore:
Ferryland

During the 1750's fishing ships from Bideford and Barnsta-
ple brought out large numbers of unskilled Irish laborers to
fish at Ferryland, Fermeuse and Renews. These ships returned to these ports on the Southern Shore because of the
utensils they had left there. In 1768, a number of Irish
servants were listed at Ferryland:

> John Brien, Ed. Murphy, Garrett Fitzgerald, Mary Shea
> Mick Power, Con Morrissey, Joseph Morey, Mike Shea Paul
> Kelly, Stephen Moores and Mick Shea.

In the same year, an Irishman from Ferryland was sentenced to death and hanged in St. John's. The hangman's fee
was 10 shillings and cost of constructing the gallows was 1
pound 10 shillings.[2]

Servants and the Nova Scotia Volunteers At Trepassey:

At Trepassey in 1775, three servants of James Jackson the
main merchant of Trepassey enlisted in the Nova Scotia
Volunteers. They were John Barrett, Martin Brennan and
Larry McDonald. Jackson complained to the governor that he
had advanced these men money and supplies towards their
fishing wages. The governor ordered the three men to return
to Trepassey and finish out their contracts with Jackson.

---

1 Head, p.89.
2 *Colonial Letterbook*, Volume 4, 1768.

Mr. Edgar Blundon

Harbour Grace

Historic Newfoundland L.E.F. English

St. John's in 1789

Chapter Five

Further Restrictions on the Irish in Newfoundland

Palliser's Anti-Papist Regulations:

In 1764 with the appointment of Sir Hugh Palliser as governor of Newfoundland, a concerted effort was made to reduce the number of Irish residing in the island. On the 31st. of October, 1764, he issued a new set of rules and regulations aimed at controlling the number of Irish Papists remaining in Newfoundland over the winter. The orders read:

> The better for preserving the peace, preventing robberies, tumultuous assemblies and other disorders of wicked, idle people remaining in the county during the winter, ordered:
>
> 1. That no Papist servants, man or woman shall remain at any place where they do not fish or serve during the summer preceding.
> 2. That not more than two Papist men shall dwell in one house during the winter except such as a have a Protestant master.
> 3. That no Papist shall keep a public house or vend liquor by retail.

4. That no person shall keep dyters during the winter.
5. That all idle and disorderly men and women be punished according to law and sent out of the country.

Every Justice of the Peace in Newfoundland was to see
that these orders were copied and posted and read in all
courthouses.[1]

Sending Irishmen back to Ireland

At St. John's, Governor Palliser seized an opportunity to
deport a number of Irishmen back to Ireland at no cost to the
governor's office. He was informed that the master of the brig
"Good Intent" had illegally carried 60 men from Newfoundland to New England. He had the captain appear before him
and on finding the report true ordered the captain to take 60
persons home to Ireland as part of his sentence

Ban on Women from Ireland Coming to Newfoundland:

An incident involving Thomas Pendergrass a servant fishing
with John Blackney of St. John's resulted in Governor Palliser
ordering a woman deported and later issuing a ban on the
arrival of women from Ireland. Thomas Pendergrass complained to the governor that Blackney had refused to pay him
his wages. The governor investigated the matter and found
that Blackney had refused to pay because Pendergrass was
involved with Blackney's female servant. The governor issued the following judgement:

> Nathanial Brooks Esq. being ye merchant who receives ye
> voyage of John Blackney is hereby ordered to pay to ye
> petitioner Thomas Pendergrass on or before the 16th, inst.,
> the wages due to him for services performed to his ship-
> ping papers in proportion to the time served without any
> deduction on account of his intercourse with a woman
> servant to the said Blackney, or appear before me on the

---

1 *Colonial Letterbook*, Volume 11,

20th., inst. as he will answer the contrary at his peril. Mr. Justice Brooks is also to order the woman who occasioned this disturbance to leave the country, and oblige the master of the ship who brought her to carry her away.[1]

The governor then issued the following regulations dealing with the arrival of women from Ireland:

Whereas great numbers of poor women are frequently brought into this country and particularly this port (St. John's) by vessels arriving from Ireland who become distressed and a charge to the inhabitants and likewise occasion much disorder and disturbance against the peace of Our Sovereign Lord the King, Notice is hereby given to all masters of vessels arriving in this country that from the first day of April next, no women are to be landed without security being given for their good behaviour and they shall not become chargeable to the inhabitants.
Hugh Palliser, July 2, 1766[2]

Too Old to Find Employment

An elderly Irishman, Thomas Grant, appeared in court in St. John's in the summer of 1767 with a request that he be returned to Ireland. He had come to Newfoundland in the spring of 1767 to look for work in the fishery. However because of his age he could not find any master willing to employ him. Now, realizing he was too old and infirm to work he wanted to return home. The governor ordered that as the captain who brought him over from Ireland had not first secured a job for him, he was not liable for his passage out. The governor secured him a passage back to Ireland.

Order to Destroy the Huts of the Irish in St. John's:

Before leaving to return home for the winter, Governor Palliser issued the following directive:

---

1 *Colonial Letterbook*, July, 1766
2 Ibid

To the Magistrates of St. John's:
Whereas a great number of hutts are erected, possessed
and inhabited by Irish Roman Catholics in this Harbour
who entertain and keep in the country a great quantity of
rogues and vagabonds to the great disturbance of the peace
and danger of His Majesty's subjects lives and to the
exceeding great prejudice of the fishing trade. You are
hereby authorized and directed immediately to pull down
such hutts or houses and suffer no more to be erected.
Hugh Palliser
October 23, 1767.[1]

This order was for the most part disregarded when the
governor returned to England, and the Irish population
continued to increase in the St. John's area.

Governor Byron's Anti-Irish Regulations:

In 1770, Governor Byron issued an edict regarding Irish
servants working in the Newfoundland fishery.

The masters of Irish servants shall pay their passage home.
No man or woman who is a Papist and did not fish or serve
in the harbour during the summer shall be permitted to
remain here during the winter. That only two who are
Roman Catholics be permitted to dwell in the same house
except such as shall have a Protestant master. No Roman
Catholic shall keep a public house or vend liquor by retail.
That the children of Roman Catholics born in this country
be baptised according to law. (Church of England).[2]

Despite the anti-Irish settlement laws, Irish men and
women continued to live in many parts of Newfoundland.
The majority of the Irish settlers were law abiding citizens,
but it was usually the court proceedings that recorded an

1   *Colonial Lettrbook*, October, 1867
2   *Colonial Letterbook*, Volume 4, p. 285.

Irish presence in the settlements outside the larger centres of St. John's and Harbour Grace.

List of Indolent Irish in St. John's area:

As the general rules governing the Irish migration failed to curtail to any great extent their growth in Newfoundland, the governor tried a new method. This was the preparing of a list of the indolent people in the island who were to be sent back to Ireland. In 1772, the Justices at St. John's prepared such a list. The persons named had no visable means of support and the governor ordered them to provide themselves with passage back to their homeland. If any were to be found after the last passenger ship sailed for Ireland, the Justices were ordered "to punish them to the utmost severity of the law." The order given was on October 20, 1772 and the people listed for return to their homeland were:

> Pat Walsh Power & Taylor, Peter Kelly & wife
> Joan Power, Widow Rawlins, Robert Whylay (alias Walsh)
> Pat Clancey, Eleanor Power, McDonald & wife
> Thomas Matthews, Old Nugent, Peter Blade (cobbler)
> Robert Flink, James Fling, John Sinnot
> Wm. Bishop (either to separate from May Hutchingson or be sent home.
> James Walsh -For opposing the constables in the execution of their duty.
> Cahill's wife and children (Cahill had been hanged October 17, in 1767)

In this same edict it was ordered that all planters and others had to pay the passage home of their servants. Also masters of passenger ships were directed to take on such persons. If men remained in the country their previous masters were responsible for any robbery or other violent act they had brought before them.

Irish Fishermen Recruited for Labrador:

However, while the governor was trying to cut down on the number of Irish in Newfoundland, George Cartwright, the famous Labrador explorer and businessman, went to Ireland recruiting Irish fishermen for his Labrador venture. He went to to visit an old friend in Ireland and notes in his diary for May 4, 1777 that:

> I went to Waterford the next morning where I purchased provisions and hired upwards of 30 fishermen for the use of my concern in Labrador.[1]

Arrival of Irish Girls:

The bringing of young girls from Ireland, first reported in 1696, continued into the late 18th century. In 1777, Governor J. Montague attempted to deal with the problems. He issued the following edict regarding Irish women:

> Whereas it has been represented to me that ships and vessels that come from Ireland frequently bring unmarried women and young girls who are destitute of friends and come over with no other view but to be hired as indentured servants that on their arrival and having hired themselves to masters have proven to be with child, which is attended with difficulties to the master and is the cause of bringing many incumberances upon the inhabitants of this island and of this place in particular.
>
> There are therefore to forbid all masters of vessels from bringing any women as servants from Ireland on pain of forfeiting ten pounds for every person so found on board or that can be proved by information to have been brought over by them, and I do further declare if any woman hired to a master on shore proves to be with child at the time she was hired her master shall not pay her passage, and if

---

1 Fay,C.R., *Life and Labour in Newfoundland*, p.81.

discovered after he pays then he shall be refunded his money.[1]

Despite the best attempts to curtail their arrival the Irish continued to come, recruited by some of the fishing firms established in the island.

Irish Youngsters Preferred:

An entry in 1788 in the Letterbook of Saunders and Sweetman, a Placentia firm, speaks well of the Irish "boys."

> We have been very lucky in having no runaways this spring, we have lost but two men and an English boy. I would advise you to never send out more English youngsters than will clear the vessels. The most of all that ran away from here, the winter before this were English youngsters and boys. They never care any of them to stick to the place, or have any attachment to it; but for hard labour an Irish youngster is worth a dozen of them.[2]

Of course, Saunders and Sweetman were an Irish based firm, and by 1790, Placentia was made up of mostly people of Irish descent. This may be the reason that the English "youngsters," far outnumbered by the Irish, didn't want to stay there.

In September of 1794, the Irish of Placentia flocked to join the militia which had been organized to defend their harbour against any enemy attacks. The list of subscribers included many of the Irish inhabitants of the town.[3]

The local militia was deemed necessary in view of the fact that for a number of years the soldiers at the Placentia fort had been reduced to about forty men. In 1798, Fort Frederick at Placentia received more troops when soldiers from the 6th Regiment arrived under the command of Captain O'Ken-

---

1 *Colonial Lettrbook*, October 10, 1777
2 *Letterbook, Saunders and Sweetman*, Dr. Hunter Library, St. John's.
3 See Appendix for list of names.

nedy. He found the poor condition of the existing fort too much for his soldiers and quartered them on the citizens. There were no complaints about quartering the men and everything worked well until they were replaced by the "Royal Nova Scotia Fencibles." This regiment proved very unpopular as they were accused of trepanning men for "the King's shilling." Pat Donahue of Placentia was fined forty shillings for saying publicly that the officers of that regiment "must be hungry sons of bitches to trepann a man for $3.00," this being their payment for each new recruit.

More Irish Youngsters Required for Newfoundland:

In 1790, the English firm of Newman & Hunt were also looking for Irish youngsters for their Newfoundland operation. They wrote to James Downing, their agent at Sligo, Ireland about recruiting Irish "youngsters":

> Consult with Mr. Hume how you are to proceed to get youngsters. Endeavour to ship for our use twenty healthy, strong men, to whom you may give from 6 to 8 pounds, and their passage out to be clear now, and if you get them to ship for two summers and one winter, that is to be clear, November 1798, you may give them 15 pounds, which we prefer to one year's service. If you can meet with such people as a carpenter or mason or blacksmith, such people are worth 2 pounds more, the same by coopers but they must ship to be employed in the fishery not confined to their trade. If any choose to go out as passengers take them at 5 pounds each.[1]

The company was successful in recruiting many Irish youngsters who were brought out to St. John's, St. Lawrence and Harbour Breton to work in the Newman & Hunt trade.

---

1 *Newman Hunt Records*, Newfoundland, 1796. Provincial Archives

Governor Waldergrave and the Irish:

Governor Waldergrave was firm in trying to prevent the expansion of growth of population in St. John's and other communities. In a letter to the sheriff just before his departure for England, he gave orders forbidding any land enclosures or erections of houses during his absence. On his return, he ordered that Thomas Newman, who had put up a few sheds, be ordered to immediately pull them down. As well, James Marroty and John Fitzgerald were forbidden to erect chimneys in their sheds or even light fires in them of any kind. Waldergrave felt the continued growth of the Irish population in St. John's must be curtailed.[1]

Irish Tavern Keepers:

However, despite the restrictions on the Irish in Newfoundland many of them prospered and by 1797 had left the service of their fishing masters to become tavern keepers. A list of those licensed to operate public houses in St. John's in 1797 has many Irish names.[2]

The number of Irish in St. John's and the surrounding areas increased each year, with Irish immigration to Newfoundland reaching a peak in the first quarter of the nineteenth century, and then declining.

---

1 Ibid p. 190
2 See Appendix for list of names.

National Archives of Canada

Placentia c.1786

Chapter Six

Fights, Frays, Robberies, Riots, Rapes and Disorderly Houses

With the increasing number of Irish coming and remaining in Newfoundland, "frays" or fights between different factions became more common. As a result an increasing number of Irish men and women went to court charged with everything from illegally vending liquor to keeping a disorderly house, from fighting among themselves to, in a few cases, assaulting women. Much of the legal troubles of the Irish resulted from too much strong drink or were simply faction fights. The Irish from the different counties brought their traditional grievances, and old scores were settled in Newfoundland. They banded together in gangs and fought each other for the honour of their counties. There were the Tipperary "Clear Airs," the Waterford "Whey Bellies," the Cork "Dadyeens," the Kilkenny "Doones," and the Wexford "Yellow Bellies." One old Irishman said that they fought "for pure devilment and diversion."[1]

---

1   Prowse (1895) 402

An Irish Fray at Harbour Main:

One of the first capital cases to be tried in Nwewfoundland following the establishment of the court of Oyer and Terminer was the murder of an Irish servant killed in a drunken brawl at Harbour Main. The case was heard on July 27, 1750. At that time Lawrence Kneeves, an Irish fishing servant from County Kilkenny, was charged with the murder of James Kelly at Harbour Main on February 27, 1750. Kelly was a fellow Irish servant, From the evidence produced at the trial it appeared that Kneeves, Kelly and another servant named John Cuddy had been drinking at the house of James Moores. Kelly was getting very drunk and Cuddy told him he should go home. He started to leave, but Kneeves called him back to have one last mug of "flip"—a mixture of hot rum and spruce beer. Then, Kelly and Kneeves got into a fight. Cuddy tried to separate them, but another Irish servant named Darby Callaghan came in and encouraged the two men to fight, saying that "if anyone interfered with the fight he, Callaghan would knock him down." At this Cuddy left the house and went home. He returned fifteen minutes later to find Kelly stretched out dead on the ground.

At Kneves' trial a statement from the chief planters who had examined Kelly's body shortly after his death was presented as evidence. It read:

> This is to certify that we the undernamed persons being informed of the death of John Kelly, servant to Mr. Philip Enco, went on Friday the 27th., and examined strictly into the cause thereof and by all just circumstances and appearance do find that said Kelly was barbarously murdered and abused, his head being battered severely and his handkerchief so taut about his neck it was impossible to put a knife point between the flesh and handkerchief. Given under our hand in Harbour Main, July 27, 1750.

Roger Baite (x) his mark   Pierce Butler
William Brown   James Moores (x) his mark
Darby Cactally   Thomas Ballaine
Philip Enco (x) his mark[1]

Other evidence was produced to show that Kelly and
Kneeves had been good friends up to the time of the drunken
quarrel. The jury found Kneeves guilty of manslaughter. He
was sentenced to be burnt in the hand with the letter "R" and
ordered to be transported back to Ireland on the first ship
outward bound for that country.

The Rape of Elizabeth Melville:

There were also serious crimes committed by the Irish soldiers stationed in St. John's. One such case happened on July
8, 1751, when a servant girl named Elizabeth Melville was
gang raped by three Irish soldiers from the fort. Elizabeth had
gone strawberry picking in the woods near Rennie's Mill
River with her mistress, Ann Moore, and Ann's friend, Katherine Whyland. They were picking berries when three soldiers approached and asked what three pretty girls were
doing in the woods. Mrs. Moore spoke rather sharply, and
Katherine Whyland ran away. One soldier took Elizabeth by
the arm and swung her around saying "Damm you, you
whore, lay down." It was at this point that Mrs. Moore ran
away.

Two of the soldiers then raped Elizabeth while the third
went after her mistress. The two soldiers with Elizabeth
spoke Irish, and she said, "I will know your faces again." Then
having held her down in their turn, they took her to the river
below Mr. Keene's meadow and put her in the river. One of
then pulled out a paper and told her if she did not swear and
sign to keep silent they would drown her in the river. She told

---

1 *Colonial Letterbook*, Volume 1, July 27 1750.

them she could not read and her word was as good as an oath. They then took her out of the river and attempted to rape her again. After that they tried to persuade her to come to them again the next day, and threatened to kill her if she did not. They wanted her to exchange handkerchiefs with them, but she refused saying hers belonged to her mistress and she dare not change. One of the soldiers said, "Damm the old bitch, if we come atwart her we will kill her." They also wanted to change the ring on her finger, but she refused. Then they let her go. She found her mistress and they both went home to Elizabeth's mother. A little later that afternoon, Elizabeth, her mother and her mistress went to the garrison and laid a complaint before Governor Bradstreet. He listened to their story and, after warning Elizabeth that a man's life hung on her identification, called in Philip Coffey, Michael Ryan and William Fielding. Coffey had witnesses to show he was not in the woods at the time of the rape, and Elizabeth made no charge against him. She identified Ryan and Fielding, who were charged and brought to trial. Fielding was found guilty and Ryan was found innocent. Fielding was sentenced to be hanged but was given a Royal Pardon.[1]

A Fishing Dispute at Fermeuse:

Another row between two Irish servants ended in the death of one of them at Fermeuse in the summer of 1752. William Quinn and William Murphy were Irish servants employed in the fishery by Maurice Haggerty of Fermeuse. The affair began on the morning of July 6, 1752. Murphy and Quinn and a fellow named Byran were washing out fish to put on a flake. Quinn found fault uith the way Murphy was washing the fish, and when Murphy made some uncomplimentary comment about Quinn's ancestery, Quinn slapped him across the face with a wet fish. Murphy retaliated by slapping

1 *Colonial Letterbook*, Volume 1, July, 1751.

Quinn across the face with fish he was washing. Quinn beat Murphy over the head with a mop handle and then went to find Haggerty to complain about Murphy. While he was gone, Murphy pulled up a flake lunger and when Quinn came back he beat him about the head and crammed the lunger down his throat. Quinn died in the attack and Murphy was charged with murder. He came to trial and had to have Edward Cockeran of Fermeuse act as his translator as he spoke only Gaelic. He too was found guilty of manslaughter and ordered held in jail until deported, but he later received a royal pardon and was set free in 1753.[1]

A Christmas Fray at Bay Bulls in 1754:

On Christmas night, 1754, a row between a group of Irishmen at a house in Bay Bulls resulted in a death and a trial for murder. From this trial we learn a little of the Irish social customs of the times and how they celebrated Christmas in the outlying settlements.

According to the evidence given at the trial by Martin Doyle who was accused of stabbing Robert Garmar, the whole thing started when a mug of "Flip" was thrown on the fire and Mrs Doyle was struck in the face."Flip" was a deadly concoction of hot rum and spruce beer much favoured by the Irish.

I, Martin Doyle do hereby say that on the 25th day of December, at night, I came into my house and found Milos Keef, Martin Doyle Jr and Robert Garmar seated on a settle, the latter with a mug of flip in his hand. Milos Keef took the mug of "Flip" out of his hand and threw it on the fire observing that I lift my finger beckoning of him for so doing, the said Milos Keef then forced against me and throw'd me in the fire. I took no notice of that but the said

---

1 *Colonial Letterbook* Volume 1, August 1752

Milos Keef being intoxicated in liquor, used my apprentice in the same absurd manner, and at the same time abused by wife by striking her on the soft eye which bruised, on sight of which I laid hold of Milos Keef to put him out. I acknowledge myself somewhat in liquor at the time having been drinking at William Dunne's, and in the scuffle with him someone took hold of me from behind my back, with his hand on my handkerchief, whom I thought was Milos Keef, but not knowing the person or who also, I by shift made an advantage of gaining my knife and cut my handkerchief by which means I cleared myself of Milos Keef, and at the same time I heard them say Robert Garmar was cut, and then mention that I had cut him. I said if I had cut him, I would cure him if I could. We left off our scrimmage then and there and they sent for the doctor. I intending to go to bed having then partly undressed, when at the same time Milos Keef advanced to me with a pair of tongs in his hand, and struck me over the right eyebrow which smothered me in blood. I called out to my son and said I was murdered, and no further have I to say, so help me God![1]

One of the other witnesses called was John Bourke who had been at Doyle's house around seven or eight o'clock on Christmas Night. He had come from James Glyn's house, where he had drunk four mugs of flip. He testified that Garmar was seated with Ellis Layman on a settle in front of the fire. Robert Garmar was in liquor, and had a mug of flip in his hand from which the witness took some. Layman did not share the Flip. At the same time there was in the house Martin Doyle, his wife, Milos Keef and Martin Doyle an apprentice[2] Doyle's son John who were amusing themselves in frolicking around the house. Bourke said Garmar got up and went out to make wind and water and when he came back he was

---

1   *Colonial Letterbook* Volume 11, 1754
2   no relation to Martin Doyle the accused

wounded and all bloody. The witness said he saw a cutlass in Martin Doyle's hand which he took and gave to Doyle's son or the apprentice and then he went home.

Then John Doyle, Martin's son, gave his version of the events leading up to the wounding of Garmar.

I John Doyle, son of Martin Doyle Sr., do hereby declare on solemn oath that on the 25th day of December, my father was up to William Dunne's and there passed away the time until evening when I went with my father's apprentice to fetch him home. I found him much in liquor, he came with us about the hour of six or seven o'clock to his own house, but when I went after him there remained in the house only my mother and children and the deceased Robert Garmar, but on my return with my father and his apprentice there was Milos Keef dancing about the house and seemed to be drinking, who acknowledged that he had been up to James Glynn's house, and Robert Garmar sat at that time on the settle, but with no visible signs of hurt. I was employed in various errands about the house afterwards, but in the several intervals came in John Bourke, Ellis Layman and James Ryan. They fell to their humour of dancing and disputes arose among them, particularly while I was help- ing put the children to bed. and my mother retired to a bedroom to take care of an infant she had in her arms, at the same time I came out I found John Bourke going away which he did about a quarter of an hour afterwards, but Ellis Layman was gone before any dispute arose. Yet Milos Keef was there and continued though much in liquor before and after the fatal strife wherein the deceased suffered, and he was by strenuous forms of my father and mother—though he really wanted the bed—was by them turned by them out of doors, after he had voluntarily rose again Milos Keef did with a pair of tongs strike my father on the head and my mother likewise did receive a blow on her head but unknown to me from whom I was so incapaci- tated and frightened in the fray that happened that other

particulars might have occurred which I am a stranger to, but I have thus further to add that I was not present when the fatal blow was struck.
John Doyle[1]

Doctor Spry testified that Garmar had not been killed instantly and he had dressed his wounds, but that he died later from the wounds.

The Verdict:

The jury, after considering all the evidence, brought in a verdict of not guilty on the charges against Martin Doyle on the grounds that no one had seem him strike the fatal blow. They did however order that before being released, Doyle should pay the court charges, an unusual order when the defendant was found innocent

Irish Troubles at Harbour Grace:

In 1755 it was reported by the magistrate at Harbour Grace that the Irish Roman Catholics far outnumbered the Protestants in that town and the magistrate complained that the Roman Catholic Irish sometimes harassed their Protestant neighbours.

> Whereas it has been represented to me at a court held at Harbour Grace, at which time it did appear by evidence that George Tobyn, master of the brig, *St. Patrick*, had threatened the life of Philip Payne, merchant, and it likewise did appear that he frequently wore Irish colours and sometimes hoisted at the ensign staff and his English colours hoisted on his jack staff to bid defiance to the English and Jersey men of the harbour, and it did appear that all this was done to stir up a spirit of rebellion among the Roman Catholics of this harbour they being so far

---

1 *Colonial Letterbook*, Volume 11.

superior in number to the Protestants in so much that it is a difficult matter for them (Protestants) to bury their dead, and they have been obliged to make use of all the force they could assemble to prevent their insolence whilst they were burying their dead. We therefore think it proper to fine the said George Tobyn the sum of 10 pounds for his insolent behaviour.[1]

The court also found that Anthony Fitzgerald, master of the vessel *Simile Snow* had hoisted Irish colours with Tobyn with the intention of stirring up sedition and mutiny. They fined him five pounds.[2]

Felix McCarthy and the Harbour Grace Riot of 1765:

In 1765 there was more trouble between Mr. Justice Garland and the Irish of Harbour Grace. This time Felix McCarthy, a merchant and one of the most prominent Irish citizens of Harbour Grace, was involved. Felix McCarthy was a planter who owned two ships, the *St. Charles* and the *Elizabeth and Francis* and employed a number of Irish servants. He also acted as an agent for an English firm. McCarthy became involved with the law when Justice Garland tried to go on board the *Elizabeth and Francis* to arrest a crew member charged with being involved in a riot.

Justice Garland complained to the governor that although he had a warrant for the man's arrest, the ship's crew had risen up with muskets and other weapons and prevented him from arresting the man named in the warrant. The governor responded immediately with an order to all the military and civil authorities and all loyal subjects in and around Harbour Grace to assist the magistrate:

---

1 *Colonial Letterbook* 1755, p. 252.
2 Ibid, p.253.

You are hereby required and directed immediately to proceed on board the said ship and apprehend every man you find in her (Except the Master) and bring them to me leaving the ship in security, and give Mr. Felix McCarthy (whom I understand is owner of the vessel) notice that he may provide other men to take care of her, all those now in her being apprehended by my order for opposing the execution of my warrant.

You are also to assist Mr. Justice Garland in the execution of my warrant to him for apprehending other rioters therein named. In case you meet with the said ship under sail without Harbour Grace you are to carry her back to Harbour Grace or bring her to this place as you find most convenient.

For your Immediate and punctual Ececution of what is here directed this shall be your warrant.

Sept. 10, 1765, Hugh Palliser[1]

On September 19, 1765, Felix McCarthy and his servants Denis Neal, Aty Nagle, Dan Sherridan, Dan Leary, James Rodrigues, Mick Dunn, Andy Latmore, James Maheny, James Welsh, Darby McCarthy and William Cantwell appeared in court at St. John's with the Governor present, and the charge against them was read:

Dan Sherridan, Mick Dunne, Dan Leary, William Cantwell, Denis Neal, Aty Nagle, Andy Latmore, James Rodrigues, John Maheny belonging to the ship "Francis and Elizabeth" and James Welsh and Darby McCarthy servants to Mr. Felix McCarthy also Mr. Felix McCarthy and several other persons unknown did on the 9th instant at Harbour Grace with force of arms unlawfully riotously and routously assemble and gather themselves together to disturb the peace of our Sovereign Lord the King then and there

---

1 *Colonial Letterbook*, 1765, p. 313

assemble and gather together in and upon persons in an unlawful and rioter manner did make an asault and ill treat and other wrongs did to the said person, also on the same day the above persons with many others yet unknown to the number of thirty or upwards in a like manner arrayed with swords, clubs and guns unlawfully, riotously and routously assemble did appear in order to interupt me in the Execution of my office and many other evils did to the great disturbance of the peace of Our Lord the King and terror of his people.

Dan Sherridan, Mick Dunn and Dan Leary were not concerned in the riot with McCarthy now in custody and others, but are the persons who in opposition to His Excellency's Orders would not admit Mr. Justice Garland to enter on board the ship *Francis and Elizabeth* to apprehend Nagle and others who were in the riot.[1]

The prisoners all pleaded not guilty, but the jury found them guilty and the governor's sentence read:

That Denis Neal shall receive three dozen lashes on his bare back with a cat of nine tails at the Admiral's stage in St. John's on the 20th. instant and three dozen lashes at the Admiral's stage at Harbour Grace on or before the 25th instant, and all other offenders (Mr. Felix McCarthy excepted) shall receive at the same time at the last mentioned place one dozen lashes each.

That Mr. Felix McCarthy shall pay all the charges of the court and also a fine of thirty pounds towards building a jail at Harbour Grace to be paid into the hands of such person as I shall hereafter appoint to receive.

I also order and direct that William Cantwell shall be returned to custody of Mr. Justice Garland in order to his proceeding to enqire into the complaint exhibited against him By Ebenezer Ware as the law directs

1 Ibid 319

Given at St. John's September 19,1765 Hugh Palliser.[1]

It is very interesting to note that Felix McCarthy as a merchant received better treatment than his servants. No whipping, and when ever he is referred to in court documents it is always, "Mr. Felix McCarthy." It is obvious that McCarthy was a man of considerable wealth and influence.

The Case of Mrs Mary Power of St. John's:

In 1772, Mary Power of St. John's, a lady of Irish extraction, was convicted of the murder of her husband, Maurice Power, and sentenced to be hanged. However, at the time of her sentencing on October 14, 1772, two midwives, Elizabeth Fleming and Susanna Earles, swore that they had examined the prisoner and that she was about five months with child. Strong representation was also made to the governor that although the woman had been convicted of the murder there had been no positive evidence to prove that she had committed the crime for which she had been convicted. The governor then issued a reprieve until the King's intention towards her plea for mercy should be known. She was to be kept in prison until the King's wishes were known. On June 23, 1773, she received a full pardon and was immediately released.[2]

Forgery and House Breaking In St. John's:

In 1775, two Irishmen at St. John's, Lawrence Hallahan and Lawrence Dalton, were charged with forgery. They were found guilty: one was imprisoned at the "King's pleasure" the other was given a pardon by the govenor. Hallahan and Dalton were back in court in 1777: this time Hallahan was charged with forging a bill of exchange for eight pounds and

---

1 *Colonial Letterbook*, 1765, p. 320.
2 *Colonial Letterbook* 1772, p. 147.

passing it to George Callayan. He forged a second bill of exchange in the name of Thomas Churchward and offered it in payment to William Cannon. Lawrence Dalton forged two orders for goods and presented them to Peter Prim, a St. John's merchant.

At the same court of Oyer and Terminer, Patrick Knowlan was charged with stealing a counterpane from Peter Prim. His defence was that he was in liquor. John Cox—alias Harris—was charged with robbing the house of Owen Sullivan. Catherine Power, who appeared as a witness, stated that Cox had come to her house and offered to sell her two silver tea spoons saying he got them from William Hall.

All charged were found guilty of their crimes. Cox was given a free pardon. Knowlan was sentenced to be:

> whipped by the common whipper with a halter about your neck, that is to say you are to receive 20 lashes at the common whipping post, then to be led by the halter to the Publick Path just opposite Mr. Peter Prim's door and there receive 20 lashes as before, and then led as before to the Vice-Admiral's Beach and there to receive 20 lashes as before; to forfeit all your goods and chattels; to pay the charges of the court and to depart this island by the first vessel bound for Ireland never to return on pain of having the same punishment repeated every Monday morning; to be kept in prison till you go aboard.[1]

Lawrence Hallahan was sentenced to be hanged. The sentence was carried out on March 10, 1777.

The Fray at John Cahill's in 1776:

As was shown in the Doyle case at Bay Bulls, Irish parties could be wild affairs that sometimes ended in a fatality. One of the cases appearing in the court records of the time

---

1 Prowse p. 344

describes in some detail the events leading up to an Irish "fray" and its consequences. The "fray" took place in St. John's on October 1, 1777, and resulted in the death of John Cahill, an Irish merchant carrying on business in the town. Richard Power, "a native of Ireland" was charged with striking Cahill with a stone, giving him a wound from which he died on November 24, 1777.

At the trial it came out that there had been a lot of drinking at Cahill's house the day that he was killed, and he had many visitors. Around eight or nine o'clock some young men looked in the front window of Cahill's house, and a man named Kennedy heard Cahill cry out, "Damn you, you rascals! How dare you look in the window?" Cahill rushed out and the witness heard the sound of fighting. Later he saw some men coming with sticks in their hands. Another witness, Sam Jutsham, saw some persons go out of Cahill's house and begin to fight on the path. He saw two boys or "low men" stoop and pick up stones and hand them to the men. Then he heard Cahill call out to his boys, "If you can't get sticks, get stones." He then heard one boy say, "Master, they are Quigley's men."

The prisoner, charged with the blow that killed Cahill, said he was only passing Cahill's house and the shutters were open with a great noise within. He stopped to look and out came Cahill and struck him with a stick, as did Samuel Power. He only defended himself against the attack. The prisoner was found not guilty and discharged.

John Mahaney's Disorderly House:

John Mahaney of St. John's was brought into court on the charge of keeping a disorderly house and having arms belonging to the king in his possession. He had also publicly proclaimed his intention to resist arrest if any came to take him. This information was given by Corporal Alex Campbell of the forty-second Regiment who had gone to Mahaney's house to buy tobacco. Campbell had asked Mahaney if he feared the press gang which was roaming the streets of St. John's at this time. Mahaney's answer was that he was "afraid of no bugger that would try to take him while he had three loaded muskets and a hanger." Campbell examined one musket but found it empty. He also told the court that Mahaney went abroad at night with a sword cane.

After Campbell reported Mahaney's conversation, soldiers went to investigate and found the muskets and ammunition belonging to the fort. Mahaney could not account for how they came to be in his possession. He was found guilty, fined twenty pounds and confined to the fort. Here he got into further trouble by telling John Ellis, the constable that he "would get it" when Mahaney got out of jail. This frightened the constable and brought Mahaney back to court.

The "Fray" at John Mahaney's House:

John Mahaney also appeared in court on September 29th, 1789, together with Michael Darrigan, Thomas Burke, John Crow and Daniel Crow, the latter a "taylor" from Trinity. All were charged in the death of Cornelius Gallery during a "fray" at Mahaney's house.

Major Pringle, Chief Engineer gave evidence that he had visited John Mahaney's house the day after the "fray" and spoken with Cornelius Gallery who was in his right senses. Gallery told Major Pringle that he had gone down to Mahaney's house where he heard that John Kennedy had been beaten by some people who were drinking at Mahaney's. When he arrived people fell upon him with spades, shovels and sticks, particularly John Mahaney, the master of the house, one of the Crows, Burke and Darrigan. He blamed his death on Michael Darrigan and Thomas Burke, Darrngan having cut him with a cutlass over the head and Burke having broken his arm with a spade.

Doctor Thomas Dodd, who had treated Gallery's wounds, reported that he was called on Sunday night, October 24, 1779 to the house where Gallery resided. He found Gallery lying on a bed with "a large wound five inches long and two inches deep on the left side of his head with a large portion of the skull drove into the substance of the Brain." Gallery told the doctor that Michael Darrigan and Thomas Burke had given him the wound.

Before his death Cornelius Gallery gave the following deposition:

> I Cornelius Gallery do acknowledge before God and the world, that I do not blame John Crow, prisoner or John Mahaney not yet apprehended for my death which is sworn against them in my information of the 24th inst. I do likewise acknowledge before God which in a short time I expect to see that I blame Michael Darrigan and Thomas Burke which gave me my mortal wound. Given under my hand at St. John's Newfoundland this 27th day of October 1779 and in the 19th year of the reign of our Sovereign Lord George the Third.
> Cornelius Gallery his X mark.[1].
> Cornelius Gallery died on October 27th, 1779.

At the end of the trial the jury said that Michael Darrigan was guilty of murder, that Thomas Burke, John Mahaney, Daniel Crow were guilty of flight, and that John Crow was not guilty of murder or flight. Darrigan was sentenced to be hung and the others were ordered transported back to Ireland. Darrigan asked for a couple of days to make his peace with God which was granted and he was confined in irons to the sloop *Cygnet* in St. John's Harbour.

Darrigan managed to escape from the *Cygnet* and got as far as Bay Bulls where, after attempting to steal a small

1   Ibid

schooner, he was captured again on Christmas Eve. He was returned to St. John's and later executed.

The Irishman on the Roof:

On August 10, 1774, Mrs. Julia McLoughlin, a respectable married woman of Placentia, was in bed recovering from a recent childbirth. She heard a noise on the roof of her house and called Eliza O'Reilly her Irish maid. Eliza came and listened and said she thought it was only the cat. This didn't satisfy Mrs. McLoughlin and she told Eliza to go outside and investigate. Right at that moment a large amount of soot was dislodged from the chimney and Eliza screamed with fear. Mrs. McLoughlin jumped out of bed to go and see for herself, but at that moment part of the roof gave way and a pair of legs dangled through the hole in the roof. Eliza screamed that it must be the devil and the two women clung to each other in fear. Then, the rest of the roof caved in and Mark Furlong, an Irish servant at Placentia, fell to the floor.

He was blind drunk but uninjured in the fall. The two women got him to his feet and coaxed him to the door. He then went to a neighbour's house where he grew nasty and broke out all the windows in that house. He came back to Mrs McLoughlin's house, but she had locked the doors and wouldn't let him in. He pounded on the door for a while and then went away and came back with an axe. He then quickly proceeded to chop down the door.

On gaining entrance he chased the two frightened women around the room with the axe over his head threatening to strike them. Mrs. McLoughlin begged him not to harm her 9 day old baby and he responded by making a chop at the cradle. Mrs. McLoughlin caught up the baby and fled through the smashed door with Eliza close behind her. They took refuge in a neighbour's house until Furlong was subdued and put in jail by the constables.

At his trial Furlong's only defence was that he was drunk. He was sentenced to 100 lashes and the punishment was quickly carried out.[1]

Robbery of Keene's Store at Bonavista:

On September 30, 1773, three Irishmen, John Burke, Wilfred Ryan (alias Burke) and John Sweeney were charged with breaking into and robbing a store owned by William Keene, the magistrate at Bonavista. They were found guilty and sentenced to death, but were recommended as objects of mercy. John Burke was executed but the other two men had their sentence reduced to transportation after having to walk under the gallows with halters around their necks. The governor ordered Keene to lay a tax of 23 pounds, four shillings and nine pence on the inhabitants of the Bonavista District to pay for having kept the prisoners until their trial.

Irish Ladies Accused of Keeping Disorderly Houses:

The court records for 1780 record the activities of two enterprising Newfoundland-Irish ladies of St. John's who fell afoul of the law. Catherine Connol and Mary Power were arrested after they went on board the *O'Sean*, a vessel berthed in St. John's Harbour, under pretext of getting paid for washing they had done for the sailors and selling them some bread. However, they were reported to have brought liquor aboard the ship for the sailors. As this was forbidden by order of the governor they were arrested and hauled into court. At their trial where they stoutly maintained their innocence, they were described as "bad people," having been known to keep disorderly houses for some considerable time. They were fined ten pounds each and ordered to mend their ways.

---

1   McCarthy M. *History of Placentia*, p. 85.

Murder in Trepassey Bay:

Another case of an Irish servant attacking his master occurred in 1790, in Trepassey Bay. Captain Henry Brooks and his crew were getting bait in Trepassey Bay, when Captain Brooks had occasion to reprimand Cornelius Bryan, one of his crew members. One thing led to another and Bryan struck Captain Brooks with an axe, killing him instantly. Bryan then forced the rest of the crew to swear that they would not reveal the crime when they came into port. He tied a grapnel to the captain's body and, with the help of one other crew member, threw the body overboard. Bryan took command of the ship and sailed first to Burin, then to St. Lawrence, and on to St. Pierre. Having obtained supplies in St. Pierre he shaped his course for Nova Scotia.

During the night, unknown to Bryan, one of the crew members who was loyal to Captain Brooks changed the course and steered the ship back to St. Pierre, where he informed the authorities of the murder. Bryan and several other crew members were arrested and brought to trial. For this crime Bryan was sentenced to be hanged and his body afterwards to be hanged in chains. The other crew members who had assisted him were ordered transported. On October 25, 1791 two other Irishmen, Patrick Murphy and John Noddy were convicted of forgery and ordered to be hanged at the same time as Bryan. The sentence was carried out on October 26, 1791.[1]

Other Court Matters:

At St. John's in 1789, an Irishman, Thomas Power, formerly of the city of Waterford, Ireland, was a very active criminal around the town. During the summer of that year, Power broke into the house of William Thomas and others and stole

---

1 *Colonial Letterbook*, 1791

goods to the value of ten pounds. He was caught and brought to trial. He confessed his crime and threw himself on the mercy of the court. He was ordered to be transported for seven years. During his trial it came out that two other St. John's residents, William and Margaret Penney had received the goods stolen by Power. They were found guilty and also sentenced to seven years transportation out of Newfoundland.

The Press Gang Murder:

On October 25, 1794, a number of Irish inhabitants of St. John's became involved in an effort to rescue a number of men seized by a press gang from HMS *Boston*. This British warship was ordered to sail as convoy guard with the ships on their way to the Spanish and Portuguese markets. The crew of the *Boston* was short 14 men and her captain J.N. Morris asked the governor to post bills for fourteen volunteers. The governor expressed surprise at this request and told Captain Morris to get the needed crew members by any means in his power.

On October 24, with no volunteers and expecting to sail the next day, Captain Morris ordered two officers, Lt. Kerr and Lt. Lawry on shore with a number of sailors to bring off to the ship such men as they might find idling about. The press gang commanded by the two officers met with no interruption or riot and brought back a number of men.

The next morning, October 25, Captain Morris gave up such men as were claimed by their masters as being necessary to the fishery. There were eight men unclaimed and seeing that they would have to serve in the *Boston* anyway, volunteered to be eligible for the bounty.[1] After the ship's company had dined, Captain Morris sent Lt. Lawry with two of the new "volunteers" to get their clothes and the wages due them

---

1   A sum of money paid to men who volunteered to serve in the navy.

from their master, Mr. Noble. They went ashore in a cutter with Lt. Lawry carrying no other arms than a dirk. Lt. Lawry accompanied by four sailors and the two men went to Mr. Noble's house and the men collected their back pay and clothing without incident.

In the meantime, word got out that the press gang was on shore again, and on their way back to the *Boston*. Lt. Lawry and his party were met by a large mob of people armed with waffles and clubs. They immediately attacked the men from the *Boston* with the intention of rescuing the two "pressed" men. In the scuffle that followed, Lt. Lawry was killed.

As soon as word of this riot was reported soldiers were sent to the scene and two ringleaders of the attack, Garret Farrell and Richard Power, were arrested. A third man, William Burrows, escaped, and 50 pounds was offered for information leading to his capture.

The reward was never claimed and Burrows remained at large. St. John's was in turmoil over this riot, led, it appeared, by Irishmen. According to one report of the time, the citizens "exhibited great alarm and disquiet and businesses were shut down for fear of what might happen." The ringleaders were to be tried, but if the governor—who was on the point of leaving—left on schedule, the prisoners might be convicted, but could not be executed until the next summer when the governor returned. As a result, the Grand Jury asked Governor Wallace to remain a few extra days to see that whatever punishment was imposed was swiftly carried out as a warning to other would-be rioters. The governor agreed to delay his sailing and the wheels of justice were swiftly put in motion.

Hanged, Drawn and Quartered:

The trial of Farrell and Power proceeded quickly and on October 30, 1794, They were found guilty and sentenced to be hanged. On the same day Governor Wallace issued the order of execution. It has been suggested the order was

signed before the trial. The order of execution, besides the
death penalty, included an extra provision which Pedley,in
his History of Newfoundland, describes in these words:

> Addition to the capital penalty was made in this case for the
> first time in Newfoundland. The sheriff was ordered to
> deliver the bodies to the surgeons to be dissected and
> anatomized. Here was an instance of swift retribution. The
> criminals had been full of lusty life and riotous liberty on
> the Saturday evening. On Tuesday, they stood in peril
> before the tribunal of justice. On Wednesday they heard
> the sentence of death passed on them. On Friday they were
> dangling lifeless from the gallows and on Saturday—all
> within a week—they had probably become the mangled
> offensive material of the dissecting room.[1]

From this account, it would appear that this was the one
and only instance of "Hanging drawing and quartering"
being carried out in Newfoundland. The intent of the swift
and savage retribution that overtook Farrel and Power was to
intimidate the Irish people of St. John's into keeping the
peace during the winter.

---

1   Pedley Charles, *The History of Newfoundland*, p. 167.

Chapter Seven

Liberty of Conscience for The Irish in Newfoundland

Prior to 1784, it was a criminal act to attend mass or other Roman Catholic service in Newfoundland. This changed on October 28, 1784, when Governor J. Campbell issued the following edict

> Pursuant to the King's instructions to me you are to allow all persons inhabiting this island to have full liberty of conscience and the free exercise of such modes of worship as are not prohibited by same; provided they be content with a quiet and peaceful enjoyment of same, not giving scandal to the government.[1]

This was great news for the Irish inhabitants of Newfoundland who had been openly persecuted for attending mass in 1755, and had to practise their religion secretly, whenever an itinerant priest came their way. At Placentia, the French had established a regular parish in 1689 with a visit from Bishop St. Vallier of Quebec. This parish lasted until

---

1 *Colonial Letterbook*, 1884

1713, and then the Church of England became the official church in the island. Now, it would be legal again for Roman Catholic priests to officiate in Newfoundland.

The Years of Religious Persecution:

Apart from the open persecution in 1755 when mass was said in the Conception Bay area, there is little information on the priests who came to Newfoundland. That there may have been a priest and a Roman Catholic church in St. John's earlier than 1784 is suggested by the date 1754, found on the corner stone of the "Old Chapel" when it was demolished.[1] In 1764, Governor Palliser reported that it was said that the Roman Catholics had priests secreted among them.[2] At Placentia, Father Cain (or Kean), an Augustinian friar from County Wexford, Ireland ministered secretly to the Roman Catholics from 1770 to 1776 before returning to Ireland.

Father Cain(Kean) returned to Ireland and another itinerant priest, Father Thomas Patrick Lonergan,(Landergan) an Irish born Dominican friar came from France in 1782. After a short stay at St. John's he moved on to Placentia where he remained for three years. He was not recognized by Father O'Donel—the first Vicar Apostolic—but remained at Placentia where he gave great scandal. He was a thorn in the side to Father Burke, who was sent by Bishop O'Donel in 1785 to establish a parish there. Complaints of Lonergan's behaviour came to the governor who wrote to the magistrate at Placentia to have him deported from Newfoundland:

> St. John's
> October 19, 1785
> Sir:
> Mr. Will Saunders having represented to me that there is a
> Romanish priest named Landergan at Placentia of a very

---

1 Howley, p. 181.
2 PRO, CO, 194/17, f.10.

violent and turbulent spirit, who has given great interruption to Mr. Burke, a regular sober man of the Roman
Catholic persuasion, and that unless the former is sent out
of the country, the peace of the place is in imminent danger
of being disturbed. I desire you will cause the said Landergan to be put on board the first vessel that may sail for
England or Ireland.

I am Sir

Your Humble Servant

J. Campbell[1]

According to Father O'Donel, Father Lonergan(Landergan) was an apostate and had been publically excommunicated when he arrived at Placentia. However, he heard
confessions and carried out the other duties of a legitimate
priest. Later Father O'Donel accused him of revealing matters
heard in confession when he was drunk, and of living with
the wife of Dr. Dutton, a Protestant. Bishop Fleming says he
got in trouble for marrying a couple who had been married
before.[2] Father O'Donel travelled the Southern Shore as far
as Renews and excommunicated him in every harbour. Lonergan then moved to a shack at St. Mary's where he lived for
some time. He later went to Fogo where, according to Father
O'Donel he died in a drunken fit in a planter's house.[3] His
grave is still preserved at Fogo.

The scandals created by the itinerant priests caused three
Irish merchants, James Keating, Pat Gaul and John Commins,
who resided in Newfoundland during the summer, to petition the Bishop of London for the establishment of a legitimate Roman Catholic church in Newfoundland. After some
time, Father O'Donel O. S. F. was appointed to Newfoundland as Prefect Vicar Apostolic under the jurisdiction of the

---

1 *Colonial Letterbook*, 1785.
2 Howley, p. 181
3 Byrne, Cyril, *Gentlemen-Bishops and Faction-Fighters*, p.64,

Sacred Congregation at Rome. This placed him outside the jusisdiction of the Bishop of London who was responsible for the Roman Catholic church in the British Colonies. The new Prefect Vicar Apostolic arrived in St. John's in 1784.

Father O'Donel had his troubles in setting up the church. Many of his Irish parishioners were living in irregular relationships, many in marriages that were not deemed valid, and he had to get permission from Rome for dispensations before he could validate the marriages. Then, too, he had to contend with the priests already in residence but without jurisdiction. The problem with Father Londergan solved itself, but a Father Pat Power, a fellow Franciscan friar at Ferryland, was more difficult to solve. Father Power had a letter of recommendation from Bishop Troy of Ireland and he spoke Gaelic, the language of the majority of the Irish in Calvert and Ferryland. For some reason Bishop O'Donel refused to give him the parish of Ferryland and instead appointed Father Thomas Ewer as parish priest. Father Ewer did not speak Gaelic. Father Power stayed put and was supported by magistrate Carter, a Protestant, who delighted in the battle between the two Irish priests for the allegiance of the Roman Catholics of that area. There was a period of some reconciliation and Father Power asked to be sent to St. Mary's. Father O'Donel refused. The battle between the two Irish Franciscans went on until 1791, when O'Donel managed to get Father Power out of Newfoundland by paying his debts.

Death of Reverend Father Patrick Phelan:

One of the first Irish missionary priests to be stationed at Harbour Grace to serve Conception and Trinity Bay was Reverend Father Patrick Phelan (Whelan). Little has been recorded of Father Phelan's activities, but tradition says that he was a good and kind man who did not spare himself to bring the consolation of religion to his far flung parishioners.

In 1799, he was drowned off Baccalieu Island while returning from a parish visitation. His body was found floating on its back with his hands folded over his breast holding the pix which contained the Blessed Sacrament. He was buried at Harbour Grace. Father Ambrose Fitzpatrick succeeded Father Phelan and in 1806, Father Ewer from Ferryland succeeded him at Harbour Grace.

Restrictions on Roman Catholics:

Father O'Donel had other problems, for the granting of religious freedom did not mean that Irish Roman Catholics were welcome in Newfoundland and there were certain restrictions. Mixed marriages were frowned on by the Protestant church and no proselytes could be received under penalty of treason. When O'Donel applied to the governor for permission to build a second chapel outside St. John's he was told:

> The governor wishes to acquaint Mr. O'Donel that so far from feeling disposed to allow an increase of places of religious worship to the Roman Catholics of this island, he very seriously intends to lay those already existing under very particular restrictions. Mr. O'Donel must be sensible that it is not in the best interest of Great Britain to encourage people to winter here and he cannot be ignorant that many of the lower order of those who stay now would, if it were not for the convenience with which they obtain absolution here go home for at least once in two or three years; and the governor has been misinformed if Mr. O'Donel instead of advising them to return to Ireland does rather encourage them to winter in this colony.[1]

---

1 *Colonial Letterbook*, 1790

The Duke of Clarence—King William IV—at Placentia:

In 1784, Governor Campbell gave the Roman Catholics at Placentia permission to have mass in the court house and gave approval for the erection of a Roman Catholic chapel in the town. The Irish Roman Catholics of Placentia lost no time in procuring a site for the new church. On October 6, 1785 for the sum of twenty pounds subscribed by the Irish workers at Saunders and Sweetman, the present church site at Placentia was purchased, and was deeded on October 29, 1785. The old French cemetery was still being used by both Roman Catholics and Protestants. All this changed with the arrival of Prince William, Duke of Clarence, later King William 1V, in 1786. He was appointed as surrogate for the Placentia area and soon showed his anti-Roman Catholic sentiments. He forbade the burying of any more Roman Catholics in the old French burial ground and revoked permission to say mass in the court house. He also insulted Fr. Bourke and threatened him with treason for accepting converts to Roman Catholicism. He forbade Protestants from marrying Roman Catholics and ordered them "to have no manner of communications with that idolatrous priest, Bourke." In fact he made himself generally obnoxious to the Irish Roman Catholics of the town. Father O'Donel lodged a complaint with the governor and the prince was brought to heel. This led to the Prince making an attack on Father O'Donel and wounding him slightly in the shoulder. He also proclaimed his intention of burning down the new Roman Catholic chapel in St. John's and sent Father O'Donel into hiding for 12 days, because of a suspected plot by the prince to have him killed. The peril ceased when the prince returned to England in 1787.[1]

In 1789, Governor Milbanke wrote to the magistrates at Ferryland regarding the importance of having the two rival

---

1   Byrne, p. 60

priests at Ferryland take the oath of allegiance to the king—now modified to exclude denial of transubstantiation—before they should be permitted to exercise their duties as priests:

> As I am authorized by my commission to administer and give or cause to be administered or given the oath mentioned in the act passed in the first year. . to the security of His Majesty's person and Government to all and every person resident or abiding here. I must desire you that you will not on any account whatsoever suffer either of the R.C. Priests at Ferryland to exercise the duties of their function until they shall have taken and submitted to the same oath of which you will not fail to provide me with a copy.[1]

Despite the problems of disobedient clergy and unfriendly governors, Father O'Donel proceeded to establish parishes and attract a few dedicated priests. With the death of Father Landergan and the departure of Father Pat Power, things began to run a little more smoothly for the Vicar Apostolic. The number of Irish coming to Newfoundland continued to grow, and Roman Catholic churches were built at Harbour Grace, Placentia and Ferryland.

In 1794, the priests and and a number of lay people from each parish petitioned Rome to raise Father O'Donel to the rank of bishop. The petition was dated November, 1794 and read:

> "Given at Newfoundland, the 20th day of November A.D. 1784, Brother Edmund Bourke, Domonican Friar, Missionary of Placentia; Brother Thomas Ewer, Francisan, Missionary of Ferryland, Brother Patrick Phelan, Francisan, Harbour Grace; William Coman, Gentleman, inhabitant of St. John's; David Duggan, do.; Henry Shea, do.; Luke

---

1 *Colonial Lettrbook* 1789-92

Maddoc, do.; John Wall, do.; Timothy Ryan,do.; John Bulger, do.; Michael Mara, do.; James Power, do.; Martin Delaney, do,; Patrick Power, do.; William Mullowney, Gentleman, inhabitant of Harbour Grace; John Quarry, do.; Demetrius Hartery, do.; James Shortall, of Ferryland; John Cody do.; John Power, do.; of Great Placentia; John Kearney do.; of Little Placentia.[1]

In 1796, Father O'Donel was raised to the rank of bishop and went to Quebec to be consecrated. He returned to Newfoundland and landed at Placentia where he received a great welcome from both Roman Catholics and Protestants. As a Bishop, he could now deal more quickly with the many problems of his far flung diocese.

B.I.S. Centenary Volume

Old R.C. Chapel in St. John's, built by Bishop O'Donel

---

1   Galgay Frank, *The Life and Times of Ambrose Shea*, p.2.

Chapter Eight

The Irish Convict Ship of 1789

On July 20, 1789, the residents of St. John's were alarmed by the appearance of a large number of men and women who came overland by the path from Bay Bulls and Petty harbour. Later, the governor in a letter to W. W. Grenville dated September 20, 1789 said that the peace of the island was disturbed by a large number of male and female Irish convicts being landed on July 15, 1789 at Bay Bulls and Petty harbour. The convicts made their way to St. John's where they aroused suspicion and alarm.

The governor in his letter complained about the effect their presence had on the people of St. John's and the other principal Harbours in the island:

> Until the arrival of these wretches in the country open and professed villainy was it seems totally unknown, among the lower order of people employed in the fishery, but since their arrival frequent punishment for crimes unknown before their arrival, had taken place. [1]

---

1 *Colonial Letterbook* 1789.

In the same letter the governor described how these men and women came to St. John's from Bay Bulls and Petty Harbour. The suspicions of the magistrates were aroused and after close interrogation it appeared that these people were convicts from Ireland who had been put ashore at Bay Bulls and Petty Harbour. The total number landed was 102 men and twelve women. The magistrates's suspicions were confirmed by a sailor, Richard Robinson. He said that he had been a sailor on the *Duke of Leinster*, which had landed the people at Bay Bulls. He said they had left Dublin, Ireland on June 14th, 1789. He also said that the people were convicts for they had been brought to the ship under guard and chained during the passage out. They had arrived at Bay Bulls on July 15th. Robinson was unhappy with the way things were going on the ship and, not having signed articles, slipped away while the convicts were being landed. One of the convicts, James McGuire, told the magistrates that about 3 days out of Dublin, one of their number, a Father Tee who had been convicted of forgery, was put on a ship bound for England. McGuire also said that all the convicts except for those with money had been chained in pairs on the voyage to Newfoundland.

After they had established that the new arrivals were Irish convicts, the magistrates and merchants, with the approval of Lt. Governor Elford, decided to take the new arrivals into custody. A concentration camp was prepared on Signal Hill and the Irish convicts were confined there. Lt. Governor Elford supplied the guards, and the merchants agreed to supply enough food to feed the camp inmates until the arrival of Governor Milbanks later in the month. All went well for ten days and then the merchants cut off the food supply. The convicts became very angry and there was fear of a mutiny in the camp. Elford saved the day by supplying the camp from the army stores.

The magistrates interrogated the convicts and compiled a list containing their names, place of birth, crimes, and sentences. Some co-operated fully, others gave only their name and place of birth.[1]

On his arrival later in the summer, Governor Milbanke was presented with a petition from a committee of merchants and traders. They asked the governor to consider the dangerous state of the island from the persons now in it, particularly the persons who had been landed at Bay Bulls and Petty harbour. The committee asked the governor to consider ways of raising money to send these suspected Irish convicts back to England or Ireland. The committee suggested to the governor that he impose a tax of 10 shillings per ship engaged as a merchant ship or banker, 4 shillings per shallop and two shillings per skiff on all ships in the colony. From the money raised St. John's would bear half the cost and the rest of the island the remainder.

The plan from St. John's was rejected by the other communities and the governor then ordered each district to raise " such sums as they think proper." Ferryland was the first to accept and gave 90 pounds on October 20; the other communities agreed to follow the governor's orders and raise the necessary money to send the convicts home quickly. The governor also issued an order to all the magistrates in Newfoundland to send to St. John's all persons suspected of having escaped from the convict ship or the camp in St. John's.[2]

On September 17, 1789 the following notice was posted by order of Governor Milbanke:

Masters and Owners of ships willing to take on board as passengers and convey to England between sixty to eighty

---

1   For list of convicts and their crimes see Appendix 1.
2   Ibid

men and women and find them with 2 1/2 lbs of bread, 2 lbs of flour, 3 lbs of pork, 3 pints of peas, and 1/2 lb. of butter and 7 gallons of water each per week, are desired to deliver tenders in writing sealed and addressed to the governor at the secretary's office between the hours of ten and eleven in the forenoon. The vessel to be discharged 14 days after her arrival at Spithead or to be allowed demurrage, which is to be mentioned in the tender.
By command of the Governor
A. Graham, Secretary, 17 Sept. 1789.[1]

The contract was awarded to captain Robert Coysh of the brig *Elizabeth* and the final terms of the agreement were that 74 men and 6 women were to be embarked for return to England.[2] The governor was to provides the irons to shackle the prisoners and Captain Coysh the guards. The convicts were received on board the *Elizabeth* on October 8, 1789. The captain was ordered to treat them well and to see that their needs were provided for as laid down in the contract. However, one of the convicts due to go on the brig either escaped or died, for only seventy-three males and six females boarded the ship.

From the two lists it would appear that the following persons either died or escaped from the camp on Signal Hill before they boarded the *Elizabeth*.

Borleigh John, Grant James, Parker Peter, Riley James, Carey Darby, Hogg David, McLesse Dan, Sheridan Dan, Cashell James, Hurley John, Mooney Bart, Stewart Dan, Conway Tim, Kelly Martin, Murray Bart, Vance Lansht, Duncan Tom, Keough John, Lee Pat, Walee Pat, Farrell John, Lacey Francis, Neweham Denis, Whyler James, Gibbons Will, Lawlor John, O'Brien Charles, Walsh Tom.

---

1 Ibid
2 See Appendix for lists of names of those sent back.

After the *Elizabeth* sailed for Spithead, a few more Irish convicts were apprehended, among them a woman who was first whipped and then sent home by another ship. The sheriff's records for October 22, 1789, show that a number of Irishmen were also sent home at the same time.

Mike Quirk	passage to Ireland	2 pounds
Thomas Halleran	" "	2 pounds
For whipping and then her passage to		
Ireland, one of the women convicts		18 shillings
Morris McCarthy	passage to Ireland	3 pounds
Ed Mahoney	" "	3 pounds
Walter Dunphy	" "	3 pounds
Lundrigan	" "	2 pounds
William Malone	" "	2 pounds
Peter Dwyer	" "	2 pounds
Thomas Martin	" "	2 pounds

Paid Thomas Wakeham for the passage of 17 men, women and children sent back to Ireland by order of the justices.[1]

The departure of Wakeham's ship for Ireland did not end the convict story. On October 23, 1789 it was reported that Thomas Walsh, James Ryan, John Keeman and Patrick Lawlor had escaped from the convict prison. They had probably been sent to St. John's by one of the district magistrates and arrived after the *Elizabeth* had sailed. This incident ended the saga of the Irish convicts from the *Duke of Leinster*. The ones who escaped settled down in various areas and were never recaptured.

---

1   C.O. 196/13

*London Tavern in St.John's where the Benevolent Irish Society
was founded*

Chapter Nine

The Planned Irish Uprising of 1800

The failure of the United Irish Uprising of 1798 brought many Irish men and women to Newfoundland. Some of these Irish emigrants had been members of the United Irish Movement, and they established the movement in Newfoundland. Among the members were a number of soldiers in the Royal Newfoundland Regiment. This was a local volunteer regiment of some 600 soldiers, the majority of whom were of Irish descent. The members of the United Irish Brotherhood were sworn to secrecy by the following oath which consisted of three parts:

1st. By the Almighty Power above I do persevere to join the Irishmen in this place. (he kisses the book).
2nd. I do persevere never to divulge the secrets made known to me.
3rd. I do persevere to aid and assist the heads of the same, of any religion : Here the new recruit kissed the book.

Although the evidence is sketchy it would appear that Father Bourke of Placentia was in some way involved in the United Irish Uprising. When the rebellion was put down, he feared some reprisal and left Placentia rather hurriedly for

Halifax. Bishop O'Donel in a letter to the Bishop of Quebec in May of 1799, mentions that one of the leaders of the United Irish uprising imprisoned in a castle in Scotland was "Sweetman the Merchant." As Sweetman had a business in Placentia it may be through this connection that Father Bourke felt he might be compromised.

In June 1798, just after the suppression of the United Irish Uprising of '98, Governor Waldegrave wrote a letter to the Duke of Portland asking that the Chief Justice of Newfoundland be required to remain at his post in Newfoundland during the winter:

> May I be permitted to represent to your Grace, that no such indulgence can be granted for the present without a risk of its being attended with the most fatal consequences to the Island of Newfoundland. Your Grace is well acquainted that nearly nine-tenths of the inhabitants of this island are either natives of Ireland or immediate descendants from them and that the whole of these are of the Roman Catholic persuasion. As the Royal Newfoundland Regiment has been raised in the island, it is needless for me to endeavour to point out the small proportion that the native English bear to the Irish in this body of men. I think it necessary to mention this circumstance, in order to show your Grace how little dependence could be placed on the military in case of any civil commotion in the town of St. John's. It is therefore to the wise and vigilant administration of the civil power we must look to preserve peace and good order (the present times considered), in this settlement.[1]

Two years later in 1800, Waldegrave's fears were justified when the United Irishmen of the St. John's garrison conspired to kill their officers and take over the island.

---

1 Pedley p. 186.

The United Irish Movement grew in Newfoundland and by February, 1800, the leaders of the group felt strong enough to plan an uprising. According to one account they intended to murder the local English Protestant authorities, the merchants and their supporters. Then, according to one plan they would invite Bishop O'Donel to become President of the Republic of Newfoundland.[1] Another story was that having looted the city they intended to take refuge in the United States. Later, in a letter to the Bishop of Quebec, Bishop O'Donel wrote that the soldiers of the Royal Newfoundland Regiment who were members of the United Irish movement were to meet at mass on April 20th, 1800. From there they were to proceed to the Protestant church and make prisoners of all that were at service there , but there is no mention of murdering them.[2] However, the good bishop is silent on his part in bringing the plot to the attention of the authorities in time to prevent the planned uprising from taking place. Tradition has it that a servant girl from Ferryland informed the bishop of the rebels' plans, and he went immediately to warn Major General Skerret of the impending danger. Pedley in his *History of Newfoundland* writes:

> As the time for the projected crime drew near, Major-General Skerret at the head of the mutinous regiment, and holding chief authority in St. John's in the absence of the governor (for it was April—months before the usual time of the arrival of his Excellency), had information given to him of what was in preparation. How that information first leaked out there is no authentic evidence to show. It is said to have been conveyed from Ferryland. But all the testimony on the matter concurs in assigning to the Roman Catholic Bishop O'Donel the credit of acquainting Major—General Skerret of the danger which was impending

1 Byrne, Cyril, *Gentlemen-Bishops and Faction Fighters*, p.144
2 Byrne, p.172.

and of cordially and most useful aiding to counteract the
plot and to prevent the outbreak, urging the major to deal
with the soldiers and undertaking himself to deal with the
misguided populace.[1]

True to his promise, when Skerret arrested the ringleaders of the proposed uprising. Bishop O'Donel, through
private and public exhortations calmed the excited Irish
populations of St. John's and prevented them from coming
to the support of the rebels. Howley does not go into detail
about the bishop's source of information, but Pedley specu-
lated that it might have come from the confessional.

> The ultimate aim of the conspirators was not made known,
> as their guilty enterprise was nipped in the bud. As the
> knowledge of the Bishop concerning it was doubtless
> derived from the confidential communications of the con-
> fessional, it was not expected it would be published by
> him.[2]

However, despite Pedley's speculation there is no record
of how Bishop O'Donel came by his information. Later in a
letter requesting a pension from the British Government,
Bishop O'Donel spoke in very unfavourable terms of his
Newfoundland-Irish flock:

> Loyalty and services have been approved of, and fully
> acknowledged by every governor and particularly Major-
> General Skerret who found himself under great embarrass-
> ment in 1799 (1800?) as having no force by land or sea to
> oppose a most dangerous conspiracy formed against all the
> people of property in this island. Petitioner was fortunate
> enough to bring the maddened scum of the people to cool

---

1   Pedley, *History of Newfoundland*, p. 216
2   Ibid.

reflection and dispersed the dangerous cloud that was ready burst on the head of the principal inhabitants of this town, and even of the whole island; for which he often received the thanks of the very deluded people who were led into this dark design of robbery and assassination.[1]

If the story is true that the leaders of the uprising planned on getting support from O'Donel and creating him President of the Republic of Newfoundland, they didn't know their bishop very well. O'Donel had a horror bordering on the fanatical of all revolutions and uprisings. This can be clearly seen from his account of his feelings on seeing some revolutionary French soldiers come to mass in his chapel:

> We had 300 French prisoners here during the summer. Their officers were at liberty, and I must own that I did not like to see them coming every Sunday to my chapel with large emblems of infidelity and rebellion plastered on their hats. It was much more pleasing to see three companies of our volunteers headed by Protestant officers, with fifes and drums coming to chapel to be instructed in the duties of religion and loyalty.[2]

Bishop O'Donel got his pension when he retired, a rather beggarly fifty pounds a year from the British Government. After O'Donel, the British government approved a salary of seventy-five pounds per year for the Roman Catholic Bishop of Newfoundland.

On April 30th, only a few days after the failed uprising, William Adams, a young officer of the regiment, wrote to his father in England. He said that all the officers and merchants were to have been assassinated "by some hundreds of the Irish inhabitants," who were involved in the plot. Only fifty

---

1   Pedley 216.
2   Howley, p. 194.

soldiers in his regiment were involved. He claimed he had been suspicious and had said so to the governor. In his opinion all the Irish vagabonds should be sent out of the country every autumn. He said that their oaths were secret and they had been sworn to betray their dearest friends to support the United Irishmen. The pass word on the 24th was to have been "Liberty or Death."

Captain Tremblett's Account of the Planned Uprising:

An eye witness account of the affair, Captain Tremblett of the Royal Newfoundland Regiment, wrote to his father in Ireland on the day of the attempted uprising:

> Since the rebellion began in Ireland their emissaries have been administering oaths to the Irish in every part of the Island. If the miscreants go to extremities you shall have no cause to blush for me.

He added a postscript to the letter to the effect that if they came through and got help from Halifax then "Pat in town will be quiet in the future." On May 2, 1800 Captain Tremblett wrote a more detailed account of the affair to a friend living in England.

St. John's, 2nd May, 1800

> Dear Lamb,
>
> Contrary winds having detained the vessel from sailing gives me time to write you, the last vessel which arrived here in the winter brought a rumour that our Army in Holland were prisoners, that Bonaparte was in France, and the combined Fleet at sea, and that the Irish determined against the Union, this spurred the villains here from that country to redouble their machinations, and they were to have destroyed all who were not of this party—they got fifty Troops to join them and they were to watch an opportunity to Strike a blow which would send us all to the Shades. I

was well acquainted with their designs but when I heard the news from England contradictory to what I have stated I must confess I was in hopes they would have been intimated, I contrived to have command on the Heights called Signal Hill with two companies, one of which I had reason to suspect, who of course I kept as much as possible from the town, it is remarkable that the ringleader of them having been guilty of a crime, that of going into town without leave twice I confined him and two nearly as bad as himself this was on the 23rd April—now the Troops go to Divine worship every Sunday—the English to Church the Irish to Chapel—and the 20th. April was the day they were to surround the Church and settle the business, the Troops formed that morning at the time of the parade, but it being a fine day, and some of our regiment (and I now recollect they were those who being in the plot must have had their thoughts otherwise employed) going thro' their exercise in a careless manner, General Skerret kept our Regiment at exercises all that day—this saved us—five or six of the rogues continued idle and dirty. I reported them to the Com'g Officer—and their second in command in mischief was confined for being drunk on the 23rd and I told him and the others that evening that I would see they had Justice done them.—by this they from conscious guilt concluded I knew their scheme and on the 24th April being Muster day, all the Regiment met when I fancy those miscreants told the others that they were discovered and that they had no Safety but in flight—fifty of them were to desert that night at about 12 0'Clock. Ten or twelve quitted Signal Hill, I discovered it about two to three minutes after they were gone and gave the alarm -, so that only about twenty got off, the others had not time—about ten of the deserters are since taken, and eight or nine of their Muskets, the rest since are in persuet of [them] and those who did not desert are snug in irons.

I am acquainted with their words, signs, tokens oaths, etc, and if it be possible worse than what we hear was in Ireland and America—the Oaths increase the turpitude, as they find the people capable of and trustworthy in this style of illumination this business has been set on foot by emiceries sent out from Ireland but as we have weeded the Regiment I fancy Pat in town will be quiet in future. I dare say we shall have troops immediately from Halifax, and we may soon expect some frigates—however if they let Pat remain in the Island this winter it will be their own fault—if he does any mischief however they must be as wise as they are wicked if they catch us off guard.

Our Old General is as good a hand as we could have on such an occasion. [1]

Another more detailed account was sent to Governor Waldegrave by Jonathan Ogden. He wrote on July 2, 1800, by which time the Irish conspirators had met their fate on Citadel Hill at Halifax. Ogden wrote:

St. John's, Newfoundland
July 2, 1800

Sir, I am sorry to inform you that a spirit of disaffection to our Government has manifested itself here last winter and in the spring. The first symptons made their appearance about the latter end of February, by some anonymous papers posted up in the night, threatening the persons and property of the magistrates, if they persisted in enforcing a proclamation they had published, respecting hogs going at large, contrary to a presentment of the grand jury. We advertised a hundred guineas reward for the discovery of the author or authors, and the inhabitants viewing it in a very proper light, as the commencement of anarchy and confusion and destruction of all order, handsomely came forward in support of the magistrates and offered two hundred guineas more, but I am sorry to say without effect. The next step still more alarming was a combination of

---

1   Webber David, *Skinner's Fencibles*, pp.64-65

between forty and fifty of the Royal Newfoundland Regiment, to desert with their arms, with a declared intention, as appeared by a letter left behind them, of putting every person to death who should attempt to oppose them. This they put into execution on the night of the 25th of April. Their place of rendevous was the powder shed, back of Fort Townshend, at 11:00 o'clock at night but were not joined in time from Fort Townshend or Fort William. We know not the reason why the party from Fort Townshend did not join them, but at Fort William, Colonel Skinner happened to have a party at his house very late that night preventing the possibility of their going out unperceived at the appointed hour, and the alarm being made at Signal Hill for those who quitted that post, the plot was blown when only nineteen were met, who immediately set off for the woods, but from the vigilance and activity used in their pursuit, in about ten days or a fortnight, sixteen of them were taken, two or three of whom informed against the others, and implicated upwards of twenty more, who had not only agreed to desert, but had taken the oath of United Irishmen, administered by an archvillian Murphy, who belonged to the Regiment, and one of the deserters, who with a sergeant Kelly, and a private, have not yet been taken. We do not know nor is it possible to ascertain, how far this defection and the united oaths extends through the Regiment. General Skerret ordered a general court martial upon twelve of those taken, five of whom were sentenced to be hanged and seven to be shot; the former were executed on a gallows erected upon the spot where they met at the powder shed, the other seven were sent to Halifax to be further dealt with as His Royal Highness should think proper, those also implicated by the king's evidence were sent in irons to Halifax; and the Duke of Kent has at length removed the Regiment, except for two companies of picked men, to head quarters and has relieved them by the whole of the 66th regiment, who are now here. various have been the reports on this business; the town to the amount of 2, 3 or 400 men mentioned as

privy or concerned in this business, and of acting in concert
with them, as least so far as to destroy and plunder, and set
off for the States, but no names have been particularly
mentioned, so as to bring the proof home. In fact we were
at one time in such a situation, as we knew not whom we
could depend on for support in case of resistance, having
every reason to believe the defection was very extensive,
not only through the regiment, but through the inhabitants
of this and all the outharbours, particularly to the Southward (Southern Shore) almost to a man have taken the
United Oaths, which is, " to be true to the old cause, and to
follow their heads of whatsoever denomination." Although
these heads are not to be known to them till the moment a
plan is to be put into action, all this one of the evidences
has declard has originated from letters received from Ireland. Although a United Irishman he was yet but a novice
and was not let so far into the secret as to know who the
letters were addressed to, or who from. Although we are at
present without any immediate apprehension of danger
we have no reason to suppose their dispositions have
changed or that their plans of plunder, burning etc. are
given up, but only waiting a proper opportunity to break-
forth. The most probable time for such an event would be
towards the close of the winter, when the ships of war are
absent, the peaceable well disposed part of the community
off their guard, and no possibility of succour for two or
three months, or even conveying intelligence of our situation. If such has been their plan, of which there is little
room left for doubt, though I believe more for motives of
plunder than of conquest, either of which would be
equally destructive, it would be absurd to suppose it might
not take place again—I should therefore imagine it be-
hoves the Government not to risk another winter, without
obviating its possible effect; and I am firmly of the opinion,
after taking the whole of what has passed into view, that the
security of trade and fishery, nay, the security and salvation
of the island itself will entirely depend upon a proper
miltary force at this place with sufficient strength to afford

small detachments to some of the out harbours to the southward to watch their motions, and assist the magistrates when necessary. This force to render a security effectual cannot be less than 800 or 1,000 men, particularly while Ireland is in such a state of ferment as it has been and is likely to continue till the business of the Union is settled, for the events in Ireland have heretofore and will in a great measure govern the sentiments and actions of the far greater majority of the people in this country.

I omitted observing that the regiment now here (the 66th) have but little more than half their complement of men, and are mostly composed of drafts from the Irish Brigade sent three or four years ago to Halifax, of course not so well adapted for the protection required, as a full and complete regiment from England, staunch and well-affected.

I have thus ventured to offer my opinion upon the public situation of affairs in this island, and have only to regret in common with the real well-wishers to its prosperity, that by the triennial mode of appointing governors we are to be deprived of the aid of your influence and counsel, at a time when from your real knowledge of the island and its internal affairs, they might be of essential service.

To the honourable	I have the
Vice-Admiral	Honour to be
Waldegrave	& etc. Sir J. Odgen[1]

On July 1st 1800, the Nova Scotia *Royal Gazette* announced the arrival of the Newfoundland Regiment including the mutineers sent to the Duke of Kent for punishment. For eleven of them the sentence was death and the Duke ordered that they be executed before the whole garrison on Citadel Hill. With the first light of dawn on July 7th, a military band paraded through the streets of Halifax playing funeral

---

1   Pedley, appendix pp. 476-478

marches and behind them followed a cart draped in black
cloth carrying eleven black coffins. Behind the cart hobbled
eleven members of the Royal Newfoundland Regiment in
chains, convicted of mutiny. They were closely guarded by
a number of Halifax regiments. At Fort George on Citadel Hill
the whole garrison and hundreds of Halifax citizens waited to
watch the execution.[1]

However, the Duke to show his liberality, commuted the
death sentence of eight of the mutineers to life imprisonment; three

others had to pay with their lives. They were quickly
strung-up and by 6:40 a.m. were pronounced dead. So ended
the last chapter in the abortive Irish Uprising of 1800. As for
Kelly and Murphy and the unnamed private, they were never
taken, and nothing further is known of them. A strong local
tradition says that they escaped to an out harbour and settled
down under assumed names.

The Royal Newfoundland Regiment remained in Halifax
until 1802 when together with a number of other Colonial
Regiments they were disbanded. On their release from the
army, many of the former members of the Royal Newfoundland Regiment settled down in various parts of Nova Scotia,
and never again became entangled with the law.

---

1   Webber, p.68.

Chapter Ten

The Newfoundland Irish in the Nineteenth Century

The failed United Irish revolt in Newfoundland had little effect on the general Irish population of the island. Although, about 200 or more Irish servants were suspected of being sympathetic to the aims of the mutineers, there was no proof that they were involved and no action was taken against them. Because the captured men were taken to Halifax for trial and execution, the abortive revolt was soon forgotten.

At the beginning of the nineteenth century, social and political conditions in Newfoundland were still in a state of transition. Although religious toleration had been granted in 1784, the laws restricting land tenure were still on the books and as late as 1808 Governor Holloway wrote:

> I cannot but lament that it was ever recommended to His Majesty's Ministers by my predecessors to grant leases of land in this island, it was striking at the root of the law which for many years regulated the fisheries as a nursery for seamen.[1]

---

1   Murphy James, *The Colony Of Newfoundland*, p.4

In a reply at the same time to a citizen of Harbour Grace seeking permission to build a house, Governor Holloway's secretary wrote:

> I am to inform you that such a request cannot be complied with as it would tend greatly towards colonization. [1]

The Irish in Fortune Bay:

Around the turn of the nineteenth century, Irish names begin to crop up in the lists of youngsters and sailors on the Newman & Hunt ships coming to Harbour Breton, Fortune Bay. Among the Irish names listed are Cox, Hickey, Hynes, McCarthy, Mitchell, Hackett and Clark: names which are found in the various communities in Fortune Bay to this day. Once in Newfoundland these Irish youngsters were usually handed on to Newman's dealers or planters in both Fortune and Placentia Bay. Many of them married their master's daughters and remained in Newfoundland as servants in the fishery.

Irish in Belleoram:

In 1800, Captain Falks, a British naval officer, made a tour of the South Coast and reported only a few Irish inhabitants in Fortune Bay. One of them however, named Owen Kenchely (Kinsella) of Belleoram, brought attention to himself, and the naval officer had this to say in his report:

> The people in this bay seem pretty quiet, no complaints of magnitude. There is one character troublesome however in the bay (an Irishman) it appears that when he drinks he seems very dissatisfied and behaves in a disorderly way and takes great pains to get others to join him, but there being few Irish in the bay, and he about 50 years old with a wife and two children. [2]

---

1   Ibid.

Captain Falks informed the governor that he had threatened Kenchely with deportation to the West Indies if he created any more public disturbances.

Petition From Fogo Island:

A petition from Fogo Island, complaining of the merchants' system of pricing goods and fish, was sent to Governor Gower around 1804.

> For a number of years back we have been struggling with the world, as we suppose, through the imposition of the merchants and their agents by their exorbitant prices on shop goods and provisions, by which means we are from year to year held in debt so as not daring to find fault, fearing we may starve at the approach of every winter. We being at the distance of seventy leagues from the Capitol, where we suppose they arrogate to themselves a power not warranted by any law, in selling to us every article of theirs at any price they think fit, and taking from us the produce of a whole year at whatever price they think fit to give. They take it on themselves to price their own goods and ours also as they think most convenient to them.

A number of Irish settlers signed this petition. They included Patrick Murray, Peter Fowler, Toby McGrath, Michael Burke, James Meehan, John Geary, William Broders and William Keefe.[1]

In reply to this and other petitions Governor Gower ordered that the merchants post the prices of the goods sold in their store and price to be paid for fish and oil.

---

2 *Colonial Letterbook*, Volume 16,
1 Prowse (1895) p. 379.

The Irish On The Cape Shore:

The Cape Shore was generally settled by Irish youngsters brought out from Ireland by the firm of Sweetman in Placentia. Branch, is said to have been first settled around 1790, by Thomas Nash, who first resided at Calvert on the Southern Shore. After he settled at Branch, other Irishmen from Placentia came and settled down there.

John Skerry, who had been brought out from Ireland by the Placentia firm of Sweetman in 1768, and fished thirty-four years in the area, petitioned in 1802 for land in Ship Cove, ten miles down the Cape Shore. He received a grant to the land he required. All the inhabitants of Ship Cove are said to be descendants of this original settler. The Irish on the Cape Shore came mainly from Wexford, Waterford, and Tipperary.

The Irish At King's Cove, Bonavista Bay:

The first Irish settler in King's Cove appears to have been James Sullivan an Irish immigrant who established a Fishing Room at Ryder's Harbour on the back of Trinity. Around 1770 he moved to King's Cove. An Irish trader know as "Daddy Yeo" had a small business in King's Cove before 1800. He sold his property to a man named Green in 1802. However, most of the Irish settlers at King's Cove came in the first quarter of the nineteenth century. These first Irish settlers were:

Ned Barron	Thomas Long	Michael Costello
Thomas Lawton	Thomas Brien	Philip Kerrivan
Paddy Pendergast	Jimmy Carrol	Pat Dwyer
Matthew Freeny	Jim Kane	Michael Murphy
George Connolly	Mike C. Walsh	Maurice Devine
Dan Whelan	John Carroll	Paddy Troy
Wm. McGrath	Tom Walsh	Richard Carroll
Mick Callahan		

In 1796 James McBraire, an Irish Protestant merchant of St. John's, established a branch of his business at King's Cove. McBraire's agent at King's Cove was Michael Murphy, a native of Waterford, Ireland. After Murphy's death in 1823, McBraire's agent was Esmond J. Mullowney from Cork.

In 1804, Governor Gower had a list made of the fishing rooms in King's Cove: The owners were:

James Ray	William Dicks	Edward Green
Thomas Walsh	Brown & Hancock	James Alyward
James Sullivan	Richard Hancock	Patrick Ryan[1]

Besides the Irish settlers at King's Cove there were about 40 other Irish settlers in the near-by settlements of Broad Cove (Duntara) and Keels. They too had come to Newfoundland in the years between 1800-1830. Most of these Irishmen had been farmers but they soon adapted to fishing. There were also a number of tradesmen among these early Irish settlers, for example, Connors and Lawton were coopers and Tom Brien was a blacksmith.[2]

Irish Settler killed by Beothucks at Sandy Cove:

On June 9, 1809, Michael Turpin, an Irish-born resident of Tilting, Fogo Island, and several other men were planting their gardens at Sandy Cove, a few miles from Tilting. As there had been little trouble with the native Indians for some years they did not carry firearms. As they went about their work, a Beothuck hunting party attacked them. Turpin's companions made it back to Tilting with the Indians in hot pursuit. Turpin's escape route was cut off and in a vain attempt to save his life he climbed upon a large boulder. The Indians however climbed the rock and cut off his head. An old Tilting

---

1 Devine & Lawton, *History of King's Cove* , p.5
2 Ibid p.7

tradition has it that Turpin's companions were saved by a woman known as the widow McGrath who came to the men's assistance with a gun and frightened off the attackers. Turpin was one of the last white men to be killed by a Beothuck raiding party.[1]

St. John's at the Turn of the Century:

In 1802 St. John's had a population of 3420, of whom 1,139 were Protestants and 2,281 were Roman Catholic. In 1807 a large influx of Irish Immigrants to St. John's brought the population to 5,000. At this time, St. John's was a very irregular, straggling kind of place. It was not laid out on any plan or system, and the houses, most of them of a very primitive character, were scattered everywhere. The lower part of the town around the waterfront was given over to the fishery and was composed of "rooms" stages and flakes. The main public buildings in the town consisted of the Court House, Custom House, Protestant church and Roman Catholic chapel. The city also contained a garrison of about 700 soldiers, and there was a strong body of volunteers under Major Macbraire, a Protestant Irish merchant.[2]

Living Conditions of the Poor, Aggravated by Irish Immigrants:

Describing the living conditions in St. John's around 1807, Mr. J.W. Withers wrote that:

> The people were over-crowded in dirty tenements, sickness was rife to an appalling extent, children were growing up in ignorance and depravity because there were no public schools to keep them off the street, and there was no hospital for the treatment of the sick. Directly of course this condition of things was due to the character of the people, their thriftlessness and dissipated habits. With them as one

1 Kinsella Joseph, *The Tilting Expatriate*, Volume 11.
2 *Colonial Letterbook*, Volume 16, 1802.

old Governor said "rum was no luxury but a necessity," but indirectly it was due to the arrival in town of swarms of poor Irish folks who were led to believe by the vessel owners who made money out of their passage, that Newfoundland was a land flowing with milk and honey. They were quickly disillusioned but could not return without assistance. The over-crowding increased, and all the evils of over-crowding both moral and physical were intensified.[1]

The Founding of the Benevolent Irish Society:

Because of the poverty and terrible living conditions of the poorer class of Irish in St. John's, a number of prominent Irish citizens of the town decided to form an organization to help their less fortunate countrymen. On February 5, 1806, a notable gathering of the most prominent Roman Catholic and Protestant merchants, military men and prominent citizens of Irish descent met at the London Inn and there laid the groundwork for the foundation of the Benevolent Irish Society. A committee was struck which included Lieutenant-Colonel John Murray, James MacBraire, John MacKellop, Joseph Church, and Captain Winckworth Tongue. They approached Bishop O'Donel and were assured of his full support.

The committee met again on February 5th., and on February 17, 1806, the first general meeting was held. Bishop O'Donel urged all the members of his congregation to fully support the aims of the new society. The Benevolent Irish Society from its beginning was non sectarian and any person of Irish ancestry could become a member. It had two main aims, Benevolence and Philanthropy, and over its nearly two hundred years of existence many a poor Irish family was relieved by its charity. Many poor children were educated at their school, originally known as the Orphan Asylum and

---

1 Mosdell H.M., *When Was That* , p.154

later as St. Patrick's Boys School. In its first year of operation the society distributed relief to the amount of 250 pounds to the poor.[1]

One of the main charitable works of the society in the early years of its foundation was to advance money to pay the passage home of the Irish youngsters who became stranded after the fishing season was over. In 1807 four Irish youngsters, Christopher Kenny, John Murray, Tobin and a fellow named Kane were helped in this way. The first executive officers of the Benevolent Irish Society elected at the February 17th Meeting were:

Capt. Winckworth Tonge	President
Lieut.-Col. John Murray	Vice-President
Mr. Joseph Church	First Assistant
Lieut. John MacKellop	Second Assistant
Mr. Henry Shea	Secretary
James MacBraire Esq	Treasurer

It was also decided that March 17th, the feast of St. Patrick, would be a day of celebration for the society.

Charitable Work of the B.I.S.:

During the years 1809-1811, the Society was very active in helping the poor and the sick as well as widows and orphans. The records of the society show that during these years they were very successful in combating the distress which prevailed throughout the town. In fact in its first 5 years of existence the Society spent 1,465 pounds on its works of mercy.

Until the fall of 1816, the Society relief was distributed in money. In that year at the quarterly November meeting it was decided that in future the relief would be given in food, not

---

1 *Centenary Volume, Benevolent Irish Society*, p.30.

money. By a happy coincidence the President of the Society at that time was an Irish Protestant merchant named James MacBraire, and it was from his store that the relief food was issued every Sunday. In 1817, MacBraire retired to Scotland. He appointed agents to carry on his buisness in Newfoundland. It was said he had amassed a large fortune in the Newfoundland trade. Although living in Scotland, he continued as President of the Benevolent Irish Society until 1823.

In 1846 the society came to the aid of the survivors of a "famine ship" from Ireland which had been wrecked on the South Coast of Newfoundland. They collectd money to help the immigrants complete their journey to the U. S. A.

Newfoundland's First Newspaper:

In 1807, John D. Ryan, an American of Irish descent, established Newfoundland's first newspaper, *The Royal Gazette and Newfoundland Advertiser*. Ryan retired in 1832 and John C. Withers took it over.

A New Roman Catholic Bishop For Newfoundland:

In 1807, Bishop O'Donel left Newfoundland and was succeeded by Bishop Patrick Lambert. He brought two Irish priests with him to serve in Newfoundland. They were Rev. A. Cleary and the Rev. Denis Kelly. Father Andrew Cleary was appointed to the parish of Placentia and served there until his death in 1829. Father Kelly did not stay, but returned to Ireland. Bishop Lambert, like Bishop O'Donel, got on well with the governor and the other prominent Protestants in the island, but due to ill health did not do much travelling. In 1811, he was successful in getting a separate Roman Catholic cemetery. Previous to this, Roman Catholics and other Protestants not of the established church were buried in the Church of England cemetery and only the Church of England incumbent could read the burial service and collect the fees.

This resulted in a number of people being buried secretly at night by their own clergy.

It was during Bishop Lambert's term of office that the British government allotted a living allowance of seventy-five pounds per year as long as he held the office of Bishop: this amount was later raised to 300 pounds per year. As well, a number of Roman Catholic churches were built to serve the Irish population in the larger outports. Two Roman Catholic churches were built in Conception Bay in 1809; one at Harbour Grace and another at Carbonear. The next year, 1810 saw the construction of a Roman Catholic church at Harbour Main to serve the people of Holyrood, Harbour Main, and Bacon Cove.

The Third Irish Roman Catholic Bishop for Newfoundland:

In 1812, Bishop Lambert brought out Father Thomas Scallan, his nephew, who served until his return to Ireland in 1815. In 1816, he was appointed coadjutor to Bishop Lambert and returned to Newfoundland. In 1816, Bishop Lambert resigned and was succeeded by his nephew.

Increased Irish Immigration:

During the next two decades, the Irish immigrants continued to arrive in greater numbers. In 1814, 7,000 Irish immigrants arrived in Newfoundland and between 1812 - 1816 St. John's again doubled its population. A record at Placentia shows that in 1813, twenty Irishmen came as passengers to that town. In 1815, there were forty-two passengers from Ireland to Placentia.

The Horror of Irish Immigrant Ships:

Some of these Irish immigrants suffered terribly during the outward voyage from overcrowding, and insufficient food and water.

On September 3, 1811, James Lannon, master of the schooner *Fanny*, appeared in court at St. John's to answer to the charge of not providing sufficient water and food for the crew and passengers of his schooner. John Lynch appeared as a witness and swore that he came as a passenger on the schooner *Fanny*. They had left Waterford, Ireland on April 23, 1811 for St. John's. Lynch was to pay 6 guineas for his passage out to Newfoundland, and gave a note in Ireland for payment. The schooner was greatly overcrowded with 184 passengers and twelve crew. He got only a quart of water from the ships's stores. For the last week of the voyage they got only a half pint of water a day. They had a forty-one day passage to Bay de Verde, and a number of passengers died during the voyage. At Bay de Verde twenty or thirty persons left the ship and did not come back.

Captain Lannon pleaded that he acted under the direction of Mr. Thomas Redmond of Waterford who supplied the vessel. He was found guilty and fined 500 pounds.

In 1815, another ship from Ireland, the 148 ton brig *Placentia*, sailed from Waterford with 153 male passengers, seventeen females and a crew of seven. As well, she carried sixty-five tons of general cargo. The only provisions provided were seventy bags of bread, and twenty-eight barrels of bad pork, part of which was thrown overboard by the passengers. Each person was allowed one quart of water per day. The passengers became so hungry they broached the cargo to save their lives.

Irish Youngsters for Newfoundland:

The Newman & Hunt Records show that in the first two decades of the nineteenth century they were bringing large numbers of Irish youngsters to St. Lawrence and Harbour Breton. An entry for 1815 reads:

We have desired between 60 and 70 youngsters be sent from Waterford in the *Resolution*. Mr. Thorn wants 20 including a master of voyage, a mason and 2 youngster coopers for St. Jervis, and if we do not get English young-sters enough, some Irish will do.[1]

The Irish continued to come to other Newfoundland communities too. Fifty landed at Placentia in 1817, and thirty more in 1818. However, the failure of the 1816-17 fishery, coupled with a disastrous fire in St. John's in 1816, made living conditions in the island desperate. During the winter of 1817, an emigrant ship became stuck in the ice near Renews and a crowd of Irish immigrants crawled on their hands and knees to shore. Many of the Irish immigrants became destitute and to relieve the situation a number were shipped back to Ireland and the other colonies with 1,000 being sent to Halifax.

Irish Inhabitant at St. Georges:

In the summer of 1813, Lieutenant Edward Chapell R.N. visited St. Georges in H.M.S. *Rosamond* and spoke with an Irish inhabitant who had lived there for many years. He lived the life of a nomad and supported himself by catching and curing salmon. Later, in Ferryland, Chapell contrasted the plight of the Irish servants who were caught up in a vicious circle of dependance on their masters.

Nothing can be more deplorable than the situation of these poor Irishmen who migrate annually in great numbers from the mother country. They enter into a bond with the master of a trading vessel and promise to pay a sum of money for their passage. They must find securities in Ireland for the due observance of their agreement. On arriving in Newfoundland the passengers are released to

1   Fay, p.20.

find an employer, should they not return the Captain publishes their names and threatens to make their securities in Ireland pay. This brings them back. When they find a master he pays the passage money, but then because the servant has to take up goods to fit himself out for the fishery, he goes further in debt and becomes the slave of his master, seldom if ever being able to pay of his original debt and freeing himself from servitude.[1]

The Honest Irish:

However, despite the poverty of the Newfoundland Irish, they were generally a very honest people. Lieutenant Chappell who on first visiting Newfoundland had formed a poor opinion of them was later forced to moderate his opinion.

> Having spoken of the industry and licentiousness of the Irish fishermen (in Newfoundland), it will be no more than justice to mention an instance of honesty in one of their class. The author had been making a purchase of some trifling article, upon one of the quays in St. John's; when, in consequences of being much hurried, he was so negligent as to leave his purse and gloves upon a log of timber near the place. The town crier was authorized to offer an adequate reward for the recovery of the property; and in less than half an hour afterwards, the purse and gloves were restored to the owner by a tattered wretch, as destitute in his appearance as the meanest pauper. The purse contained about 10 pounds sterling.[2]

The Beginning of a Movement for Self Government:

With the great increase in population, and with the establishment of a newspaper, the non—sectarian Benevolent Irish Society and a regular postal service for the island, the larger outports were slowly moving towards a more regu-

---

1 Chappell Edward, Lieutenant, *Voyage of the Rosamond,* p.219.
2 Chappel Edward, Lieut, *Voyage to Newfoundland,* p. 53

lated civil life. Governor Duckworth, who became Governor in 1810, encouraged agriculture and made a number of migratory fishing rooms available to the resident population. In 1812, he advised the British Government that Newfoundland needed some form of self government. It was around this time that Dr. William Carson, a Scotsman, aided by Patrick Morris, an Irish merchant of St. John's, began the struggle for self-government for Newfoundland.

Scene in Ireland c.1800

Chapter Eleven

Faction Fights and Irish Support for an Elected Assembly

During the first quarter of the 19th century, the favourite gathering place for the Irish servants in St. John's was at the eastern end of the lower path near King's Beach and Sawyer's Corner where the National War Memorial stands today. Despite the efforts of naval officers, governors and three Roman Catholic bishops to put down faction fights, the men from the different Irish counties continued to meet there to prove their manhood.

Chief Justice Caesar Colclough and the Faction Fight of 1815:

It was at this spot early on a March morning in 1815 that the men from Tipperary, Waterford and Cork met to fight the men from Kilkenny and Wexford. The battle continued from about 7:00 a.m. until 9:00 p.m. The Chief Justice, Caesar Colclough, a Protestant Irishman, was at home sitting with his sick wife, when an old Irish servant rushed into the room saying that several constables had arrived requesting the Chief Justice to go out and put down the fight or the town would be in ruins. The Chief Justice rushed out in time to hear the guns from Fort William, Fort Townshend and Signal

Hill signal they were in readiness to put down any riots. Before the Chief Justice arrived on the scene, the faction fighters, fearing that the soldiers were on their way, had all retreated to the barrens. There General Finn stripped to fight General Muldowney for the honour of Waterford against the "yaller bellies" of Wexford. However, James McBraire, the head of the local militia force, arrived with his men. The faction fighters, who greatly feared McBraire and his long staff, fled in all directions.

Colclough, an Irishman from an old Protestant Wexford Family, took the faction fights seriously and feared a conspiracy. He arrested the leaders of the factions and charged them with disturbing the peace. The next night about 300 men assembled on the Middle Path, but the Chief Justice accompanied by the constables threatened to read the riot act and they dispersed peacefully. As a result of the March faction fight one fellow was whipped and the others imprisoned until the start of the fishery.[1]

Religious Schism:

The faction fights even caused problems in the Roman Catholic Church. When Bishop Lambert suspended one of his priests named Father Power, there was religious schism. Father Power, a native of Tipperary, was supported by that faction. Bishop Lambert, a County Wexford Man, was supported by the Wexford "Yellow Bellies." However, Father Power was retired to Long Pond. He died in 1818, and it was not until then that the schism ended.

The faction fights continued however, until the local Irish became involved in political activity. Then most battles, both verbal and physical, were reserved for the political arena. Fights also occurred when people went out as "Fools" or "Mummers" at Christmas time. It was then that many old

---

1   Murphy, Michael P. *Pathways Through Yesterday*, p. 31.

grievances were settled. "Mummering" was finally outlawed after a man was murdered in Bay Roberts.

The Winter of the Rals:

In 1817, one of the worst fishing seasons in decades brought much distress all over Newfoundland. However, in spite of the poor times, a large number of Irish immigrants continued to arrive to increase the sufferings of those unable to feed themselves. The failed fishery was followed by a great fire in St. John's in which 1700 people were left homeless. A proclamation by Governor Pickmore suggests that in some cases the fires were an attempt to settle old scores.

> Whereas it has been reported to me by the magistrates that a discovery was this day made, of a deliberate attempt to set fire to the house of William Hogan in Magotty Cove, whereby a great part of the remains of this unfortunate town would have probably been destroyed, and many of the distressed inhabitants left without shelter at the severest season of the year; and whereas this new attempt, connected with the unexplained causes of the fires of the 7th, and 21st, of November last leaves little room to doubt that there are in this community some persons of diabolical dispositions, whom no feelings of human nature can restrain from horrid crimes.[1]

The governor offered a reward of 300 pounds to anyone who helped bring these people to justice. It was a terrible winter and as Judge Prowse wrote, "famine, frost and fire combined like three avenging furies, to scourge the unfortunate island."

The Winter of the Rals Outside St. John's:
Bay Bulls

Outside St. John's the people were in an even more desperate condition and in several communities on the Southern

---

1 Pedley, Charles, Rev. *The History of Newfoundland*, p.315

Shore men and women took desperate measures to feed their starving families. In February of 1817, the brig *Guysborough* put into Bay Bulls in distress. The ship was laden with supplies and when none were shared with the starving citizens of Bay Bulls, John Mulcahey organized the men of the community to seize the ship and unload half her cargo, which was distributed among the people of the community. To prevent violence the magistrate of the area, Peter W. Carter, who was on hand, assured the captain of the *Guysborough* that the owners would be paid for the supplies taken. The governor later honoured Carter's promise. John Mulcahey, however was ordered arested for "being particularly active in the large riotous and tumultuous assembling of people at Bay Bulls" and when he was not to be found a reward of twenty pounds was posted for his capture, but he was never taken.[1]

Renews

At Renews, a mob of hungry people led by the local blacksmith attempted to seize the supplies of two English fishing crews who had been frozen up in the harbour. The attackers were driven off by musket fire, but when order was restored the fishing crews shared all their supplies with the hungry people of Renews. That same winter an Irish immigrant ship became stuck in the ice off Renews and the people crawled ashore over the ice on their hands and knees, adding to the misery of an already starving people.

The Benevolent Irish Society Founded in Conception Bay:

In 1814, Father Thomas Ewer and Dr. William Stirling R. N. founded the Irish Benevolent Society at Harbour Grace. It was known as the Bemevolent Irish Society of Conception Bay. Seventy years later an Italian born bishop tried to take control of the organization, but failed.

---

1   O'Neill, Paul, *The Seat Imperial*, p.32

The Flogging of James Landergan:

Around 1812, the first agitation for some form of elected local government for Newfopundland was begun by Dr. William Carson.

Dr. Carson, a Scotsman, was supported by the great majority of Irish, represented by Patrick Morris, an Irish born merchant of St. John's. In the summer of 1819, the leaders for self government took exception to the punishment meted out to James Landergan (Lundrigan) by a surrogate court at Harbour Grace.

James Landergan, a fisherman of Irish descent, had a fishing room at Cupids. During a couple of poor fishing seasons he became indebted to Graham and McNicoll, merchants of Harbour Grace, to the tune of fifteen pounds. He did managed to reduce the debt to twelve pounds, but in the spring of 1819 was served with a summons to appear in court at Harbour Grace for non-payment of the debt. Landergan ignored the summons and in his absence judgement was given against him, and the court ordered his property seized and sold to pay the debt.

The bailiff, Mr. Kelly, seized Landergan's boat in May. Later, while Landergan was absent from Cupids, John Moores, a Harbour Grace constable who lived at Bareneed, served a writ by attaching it to Landergan's fishing room. The bailiff, Mr. Kelly, came to seize the property, but Mrs. Landergan gave him a warm welcome. Surrounded by her small children, musket in hand, she threatened to blow his head off if he didn't get off the property quickly. Mr. Kelly fled the scene.

In the meantime the court sold Landergan's property, worth an estimated 100 pounds, to D. Graham for twelve pounds to cover the debt. On July 5, 1819, Landergan was served with a summons to appear at a surrogate's court at Port de Grave on July 6, to answer to a contempt of court charge for not appearing when summoned to appear in court at Harbour Grace in May. He was arrested and brought before the court at Port de Grave where he was found guilty as charged and ordered to receive thirty-six lashes.

The prisoner was tied to a flake and flogged by the boatswain of H.M.S. *Grasshopper*. After fourteen lashes Landergan fainted, and Dr. Richard Shea, the surgeon at Port de Grave, asked that the flogging be stopped. Landergan agreed to hand over his property without any further trouble and the court rescinded the remaining lashes.

Civil Suit for Trespassing:

This, however, was not the end of the case, for Landergan sued the two surrogate judges, Captain David Buchan R. N. of H.M.S. *Grasshopper* and the Reverend John Leigh, the Escopalian Missionary of Harbour Grace, for trespass. They now became the defendants. During the trial Dr. Shea gave evidence in support of Landergan:

> . . . was present at the Surrogate Court held there by the defendants in July last. Plantiff wa sentenced to receive 36 lashes for contempt of court in not attending according to order. Mr. Leigh silenced the plantiff and turned to Capt. Buchan who seemed to assent. The plantiff was removed from the court and held by the wrists and legs to a stake where he received 14 lashes and fainted. He was flogged by a man belonging to the *Grasshopper*, with a cat o'nine tails.[1]

The jury—as instructed by the judge—found in favour of the two surrogate judges but expressed "their abhorrence of such unmerciful and cruel punishment for so trifling an offence." The people of Newfoundland, outraged by the whole affair, showered the governor with petitions demanding changes in the administration of law in Newfoundland. Carson seized on the Landergan case to press for legal and

---

1   Fay, p.114

political reform. No other single cause united the people in their demand for some form of self-government as did the Landergan case.

At a meeting in St. John's on November 14, 1820 Carson, supported by Patrick Morris, Henry Shea, Timothy Hogan, Patrick Doyle, John Ryan, Thomas Burke, Lewis W. Ryan and others agreed to pay Landergan's court expenses and also expressed their determination to form a committee to petition the British Government for legal reform. In support of this demand a petition was presented in the British House of Lords in 1821. As a result, the question of some form of self government began to be considered by the British Government.

Surprised by the outrage of the general public, Reverend Leigh stated in November of 1820 that the punishment was inflicted "from unfortunate circumstances of gross misrepresentation" and that it was intended to indemnify Landergan by purchasing his fishing room and restoring it to him and his family.[1]

The Movement for Legal and Political Reform:

As the rather unwelcome Irish swelled the population of St. John's, the demands for reform in the legal system and for some form of elected government continued to grow. In 1820 Governor Hamilton advised the British Government that Newfoundland might now "be more properly termed a colony than a fishery plantation." The first step towards reforming the legal system was the Imperial Act of 1824 for the better Administration of justice in Newfoundland. In 1826, the Newfoundland Supreme Court was established by Royal Charter with a Chief Justice and two assistant judges. Three circuit courts, the Central, Southern and Northern were also established. In 1828, a letter by Patrick Morris, an

---

1 Fay, p. 114.

Irish merchant in St. John's, was published in London on the need for granting a constitutional government in Newfoundland. This letter was very influential in persuading the British government to give Newfoundland some form of elected assembly. Judge Prowse, a Newfoundland historian, tells a story of the time Patrick Morris tried to cross swords with the great Daniel O'Connell at a meeting in Ireland. When Morris got up to speak opposing O'Connell's views:

> O'Connell called out in his broadest Kerry brogue, "Well Pat, when did you come across, was there much fog on the Banks?" and then with finger to his nose said, "Boys do you smell the fish?"[1]

After that Morris kept to reform for Newfoundland.

Support for Elected Goverment by Bishop Fleming:

In 1829, a new and powerful voice was added to the clamour for political reform when Father Michael Anthony Fleming became the fourth Roman Catholic Bishop of Newfoundland.

---

1   Prowse (1895) 425.

Chapter Twelve

Religion, Politics, and the Newfoundland Irish

From the granting of religious tolerance to the Roman Catholic population of Newfoundland in 1774, until the consecration of Bishop M. Fleming in 1829, the Roman Catholic Church under Bishops O'Donel, Lambert and Scallan had not been actively involved in politics. The first three Roman Catholic bishops supported the establishment and kept well out of the political arena. All this changed with the appointment of Bishop Michael Anthony Fleming as coadjutor bishop to Bishop Scallan in 1829. The consecration of Bishop Fleming coincided with the passing of the "Catholic Relief Bill" in England, and the removal of all political restrictions on Roman Catholics in Newfoundland.

A Very Tolerant Bishop:

Bishop Scallan had been the most tolerant of men. He allowed his clergy to attend Protestant funerals and on occasions he remained himself in the Protestant church while prayers were read. Many Roman Catholics attended mass in the morning and then accompanied their Protestant friends to their church in the evening. As a priest Fleming had been outraged at such liberal views of religious toleration, but could do nothing until he became bishop. In fact Rome was

informed of these activities and a censure arrived condemn-
ing Bishop Scallan for his conduct. Bishop Fleming did not
inform Bishop Scallan of the censure as he was on his death
bed when it arrived. Bishop Scallan died on May 29, 1830,
and with his death the toleration he had preached and
practised came to an abrupt end. Bishop Fleming imposed a
more strict interpretation on the limits of religious toleration
and the gulf between Irish Roman Catholics and English
Protestants widened. The racial and religious differences
were to become most manifest in the political arena of the
next four decades.

The Recruitment of More Irish Priests for the Newfoundland Mission:

One of the major tasks facing Bishop Fleming in the administration of dioceses was the lack of clergymen. However, the
good bishop brought over from Ireland a number of Irish
priests who worked long and hard to establish a strong Irish
Roman Catholic presence in the Island. Among the best
remembered of these Irish priests are Father James Duffy
who served at St. Mary's, Father Berney of Burin parish and
of course Dean Patrick Cleary who for more than fifty years
laboured in the parish of Witless Bay on the Southern Shore.

Irish Support for The Final Push for An Elected Assembly:

On the 29th of September 1831, after many meetings, a
petition was drafted "To the King's Most Excellent Majesty"
from the citizens of St. John's, Newfoundland asking for "a
constitutional Legislative Government" a similar petition was
drafted for the British Parliament. As a result a committee was
formed to lobby for the resolutions contained in the petitions. Mr. Patrick Morris proposed the following persons be
on the committee. His motion was seconded by Mr. L.
O'Brien.

Dr. Carson, Messrs. Brooking, W. Thomas, Morris, Lawler, M'Bride, Bennett, John Kent, Job, Row, H. Thomas, Dr. Rochford, Messers. Doyle, C. Lilly, James Kent, Bland, J.B. Thompson, Capt. Pearl R.N.; Messers. Robert Brine and John Shea

Similar petitions supporting the one from St. John's were received from Harbour Grace, Carbonear, Port de Grave and Old Perlican.

On Tuesday, November 29, 1831, a dinner was held at Mrs. Travers' Hotel to honour Thomas Holdsworth Brooking who had been selected by the committee to take the petitions to England. The final toast drunk was to "A full free and independent representation of the people of Newfoundland in a Legislative Assembly."[1]

Bishop Fleming's Entry into the Political Field:

The mission was successful and Newfoundland had its first election in the autumn of 1832. One of the candidates who offered himself as a member for St. John's was Mr. John Kent, a recent arrival from Ireland who was later married to Bishop Fleming's sister. His candidacy was strongly opposed by Henry Winton, the Protestant editor of the *Public Ledger*. Winton felt that Kent, as a recent arrival who had not been long involved in the struggle for an elected assembly, was an upstart who should be put in his place: "an inflated schoolboy," Winton called him.

Kent took strong exception to Winton's attack and in the *Newfoundlander* a pro Irish Catholic newspaper, replied with a personal attack on Winton calling him, "This political Janua." Winton replied "that Kent was neither a gentleman nor a scholar." Kent then circulated a pamphlet which suggested that Winton was accepting Government patronage to

---

1   Smallwood, J. *Dr. William Carson* p.70

put down the people and had become the enemy of the new, soon to be elected assembly.[1] It also suggested that Winton's motive for abandoning the local cause was an uncompromising hatred of Irishmen and Catholics. This was the first mention of religious bias in Newfoundland politics. In the September 20, 1832 edition of the *Newfoundlander* Kent wrote that Winton had attacked him because he was "an Irishman and a Catholic."[2]

Winton hastened to deny the charge that he was anti-Irish or anti-Catholic, saying that his Irish-Catholic friends would support his denial of any racial or religious prejudice against the Irish or Roman Catholics. He went on to say:

"Sure we are that the Right Reverend Bishop of the church of which Mr. Kent is a member, will not tolerate such conduct."[3]

Winton was greatly mistaken. Bishop Fleming came to the aid of his future brother-in-law and denounced the editor of *The Public Ledger*. He also attacked Winton for publishing "abusive insinuations" about himself and his clergy and declared John Kent to be no less than a "protegé of the church."[4]

Winton replied with a savage personal attack on Bishop Fleming, saying Fleming had now lost the respect not only of the Protestants but also of the respectable portion of his own Catholic flock. Winton ended his article with these words:

What shall be said of you when you can so far prostitute your sacred calling to secular purposes of so unworthy a

1   Moyles R.G. *Complaints is Many and Various, but the odd Divil likes it.* p. 89.
2   *Newfoundlander*, September 20, 1832
3   Pedley, p. 380.
4   *Newfoundlander*, September 20, 1832, Bishop Fleming to Editor.

character—when you can affix the emblem of the cross to your name for the purposes of furthering your views in a mere trumpery contested election squabble... You are not beyond the influence of the press which has only begun to deal with you. In your collision with it, take care you do not overrate your own strength.[1]

Fleming replied to this very personal attack by calling a public meeting of Roman Catholics in the old chapel. Two resolutions were passed at the meeting; one expressed total veneration for Bishop Fleming, the other denounced Winton for his attack.[2] The war of words continued through the remaining few weeks of the election campaign. Unfortunately for Newfoundland, it was the beginning of a century in which religion and politics marched hand in hand.

One of the surprises of that first election was that Dr. W. Carson, who ran in St. John's with the full support of Bishop Fleming and John Kent, was defeated by a man named Keough. Judge Prowse claimed that he was defeated because of a story which aroused the old Irish faction animosities. According to Prowse:

> An Irishman called Bennett came into the booth where a number of Wexford were casting their votes. "Well," he said, "I heard the Doctor say he did not care how it went as long as he could bate Keough and them blooming 'yellow bellies.' " Mr. Keough was a Wexford man and after that he got every Wexford vote. The story was a barefaced lie, but it served its purpose.[3]

In fact Dr. Carson had to wait until a by-election was called in 1834 to win a seat. In the meantime Dr. Carson

1 Ibid. 381
2 Report of Meeting on September 27, 1832 in the October 4, edition of the *Newfoundlander*.
3 Prowse (1895) p. 430

founded a newspaper called the *Newfoundland Patriot* and
Henry Winton became his greatest enemy. In the by-election
of 1834, Winton supported the candidacy of Timothy Hogan,
an Irish Roman Catholic shop keeper and former president
of the Benevolent Irish Society. However, in the December 3,
1834, edition of the *Ledger*, Winton published the following
notice from Timothy Hogan:

> To The Independent Electors of
> The District of St John's
> Gentlemen,—The die is cast! In the hour of victory I am
> constrained to retire from the contest, and abandon the
> hope of being useful to you as your Representative.
>
> A Reverend Gentleman has announced from the sacred
> Altar, that it would promote the interest of religion to elect
> my opponent, (Dr. W. Carson) and has thundered forth in
> Prophetic anathemas that he would cause grass to grow
> before the doors of those who would vote the contrary.
>
> Thus the will of the Rev. Gentleman must be considered
> as the text of your choice in a Representative. Single-
> handed I had nothing to fear, and everything to hope, but
> in order to preserve the peace of the community which I
> very much feared would be disturbed in your struggle for
> the Purity of Election against an influence which is well
> known I was at all times unwilling to oppose. I determined
> to leave my opponent in possession of an inglorious field.
>
> Adieu my friends, I sincerely thank you for your able and
> kind exertion, and most ardently hope our common coun-
> try will not suffer by the admission into its counsels of any
> Gentleman who is not the subject of the people's choice.
> I have the honour to remain
> Gentlemen
> Your obedient servant.
> Timothy Hogan.[1]

---

1 *Public Ledger*, December 3, 1833.

Timothy Hogan's letter suggests that although a Roman Catholic, he was a rather independent person not amenable to clerical pressure while Doctor Carson had the full support of the Roman Catholic Church. It was well known that Hogan's friends were privately threatened with being cut from the sacraments if they supported him.[1] Faced with financial ruin if he opposed the Roman Catholic clergy's favourite, Hogan withdrew and apologized to the bishop, and Carson was elected by acclamation.

Following the election, Winton continued to denounce Carson, Bishop Fleming and the Roman Catholic clergy in the most inflammatory way. He summed up the political realities of the day in this article.

> To be plain the priesthood of the Roman Catholic Church in this town appear to have enlisted in the service of mammon rather than in the service of God—and the altar and the pulpit have been alike desecrated to the service of Dr. Carson and his electioneering interests and to a continued course of scandal and abuse against individuals and families both within and without the pale of her communion. Where is the spirit that once hovered over, and as it were, directed the conduct of an O'Donel and a Lambert? Is it clean gone forever! Were it possible that the glorified spirits in heaven could be rendered susceptible of pain and distress, would these not shed a thousand tears over the fallen Church of which they themselves had laid the foundation.[2]

Bishop Fleming denounced Winton from the pulpit and in the Catholic press. He also denounced the governor, Sir Thomas Cochrane for having placed government ads in *The*

---

1 Gunn, *The Political History of Newfoundland*, 1832 -1864,p.20.
2 Moles, R.G., *Complaints Is Many and Various but the odd Divil likes it*, p.96.

Public Ledger. As a result of the inflammatory articles in *The Public Ledger* and the sermons of Bishop Fleming and his priests, the house of Henry Winton was attacked on December 23, 1833 and for several nights afterwards and the military had to be called out to quell the mob whom Winton referred to as the "Pat-rioters."[1]

The use of the military angered Bishop Fleming and led to verbal abuse of Sir Thomas Cochrane by the bishop and his clergy. A bitter exchange of letters between the bishop and the governor in the St. John's press followed. Fleming accused the government of inciting riots and Cochrane defended his actions. Cochrane was accused of bigotry, injustice and despotism, and because the situation in St. John's was clearly leading to mob violence, Cochrane was removed and replaced by Governor Prescott.[2] In fact when Sir Thomas Cochrane and his daughter were passing down Cochrane Street to their ship, they were hooted by a mob who pelted their carriage with mud and stones. However, some years later even Bishop Fleming admitted that Sir Thomas Cochrane was the best governor that Newfoundland had ever had.

The Hanging Judge:

In 1833, Chief Justice Tucker resigned and was replaced by Henry Boulton, the former Attorney-General of Upper Canada. Boulton was very anti-Irish Roman Catholic and immediately became the bitter enemy of Carson, Kent and Bishop Fleming. As Chief Justice he was automatically President of the Legislative Council and could frame and then administer his own laws. He had a law passed—4 Wm. 1V, c. 5—that gave him wide discretionary powers to inflict whipping, hard labour in iron clogs or shackles, solitary confinement, as well

---

1   CO 194/85, Governor Cochrane to Lord Stanley, December 26, 1833.
2   Moyles, p.96.

as power to regulate prison discipline and diet. Judge Prowse said of Boulton:

> Boulton had undoubted ability, but he was the worst possible selection for both the Council and the Bench. His views both of law and legislation were most illiberal; as a technical lawyer he was mostly right and sublimely independent, but his harsh sentences, his indecent party spirit and his personal meanness caused him to be hated as no one else was ever hated in this colony.[1]

To the Irish who came before him he was simply the "Hanging Judge," and they felt that he had a hatred of all things Irish and Roman Catholic. This feeling was further fuelled by two separate incidents that occurred in 1835. The first was the struggle between Father James Duffy of St. Mary's and the Honourable Chief Justice over the destruction of a fish flake at St. Mary's on January 13, 1835. The second was a brutal attack on Henry Winton on Saddle Hill on May 19, 1835.

---

1   Prowse (95) p. 434.

R.C. Church at St. Mary's

Father Duffy's Well

Chapter Thirteen

St. Mary's and The Father Duffy Affair

Growth of Irish Population In St. Mary's:

Between 1760 and 1790 the Irish population of St. Mary's increased when a number of Irishmen settled there. Among the new comers were John Fagan, William Fagan, William Fewer, John Peddel, Tom Browne, and Henry Lee. By 1819, a census showed the population of St. Mary's to be 454 persons of whom 431 were Irish born or of Irish descent. There were twenty-three English Protestants, the majority of whom were the managers and their families of the English fishing companies with branches at St. Mary's. The community had sixty-three dwelling houses and three public houses kept by William Christopher, Elizabeth Fewer and Richard Critch. William Christopher was chief constable for the area. There were sixteen fishing boats employing 108 men and another sixty-four men fished in small boats from the shore. There were also seventeen fishing rooms in the community. The population of the St. Mary's was slowly increasing for in 1819 there were twelve births and three deaths.

Life at St. Mary's, like that of the other Newfoundland outport communities, revolved around the fishery. William Phippard, a merchant magistrate, and John Hill Martin, the manager of the branch store of Slade Elson, ruled the community. The court records of the day show little serious crime, but there were plenty of civil cases for non payment of debts, domestic quarrels, social problems and even one case of slander involving witchcraft.[1] In 1835, there came the famous riot and rebellion case involving Father James Duffy, John Hill Martin and Chief Justice Henry Boulton.

Father James Duffy and the Troubles of 1835:

Up until 1834, the Roman Catholic people of St. Mary's Bay had been part of the parish of Renews, with occasional visits from the priests of that parish. In 1834, Bishop Fleming established a separate Roman Catholic parish for St. Mary's and appointed Father James Duffy, a curate at Renews, as the first parish priest of the new parish.

Some years earlier the people of St. Mary's had built a chapel. However, due to its exposed position on a wind swept hill it blew down during a winter's storm. It was rebuilt on the same site, but the year before Father Duffy's arrival as parish priest, another severe winter storm destroyed the second chapel.

Father Duffy took up residence in St. Mary's in March of 1834, and his first task was to organize the building of a new chapel. Having examined the site of the old chapel carefully and talked with the residents, Father Duffy determined it was necessary to move the site of the church to a beach below the hill. The site that Father Duffy picked for his new church had always been considered common property in St. Mary's, and was used by all the fishermen of the harbour to dry and mend their nets and repair their boats. As there were no roads in the community at that time the beach also served as part of the path to the nearby community of Riverhead. However, in the

---

1   see Appendix

spring of 1834, William Fewer, a resident of St. Mary's, built a small fish flake on the beach. John Hill Martin sent his men over and cut down Fewer's flake and then had them build a flake that ran the whole length of the beach. This cut the local fishermen off from their traditional net drying access, and blocked the path to the cemetery which was located on the mound behind the beach, near the site of the old chapel.[1]

The fishermen of St. Mary's, on the advice of Father Duffy, protested Martin's seizure of the public beach. Martin claimed it was not a public beach but had been the property of a man named Doyle, who had sold it to William Christopher, and Christopher had sold it to Slade Elson which gave them title to the beach.

Father Duffy recognized John Hill Martin's authority as magistrate by asking his permission to build the new church near the beach. Martin refused permission for a beach site, but offered an alternate site. However, when Father Duffy examined the proposed site he found it was a very poor location, being both wet and marshy. He pointed out the unsuitability of the site to Martin who told him bluntly that it was that site or nothing. When it became apparent that Martin meant what he said, Father Duffy decided he would defy Martin and build the church on the beach site he had chosen.

In early November Father Duffy swore his congregation to secrecy and then sent them into the woods to cut and saw by hand all the framing and the boards needed to build the new church. In early December everything was ready to be hauled out of the woods and assembled. Duffy gave the word to go ahead. He divided the men of the parish into groups each under a captain, and while one group brought out the materials, the best carpenters in the parish began construc-

---

1   Howley M.F. Rt. Rev. *Ecclesiastical History of Newfoundland,* p.326.

tion. They started at daybreak and by noon the new church stood ready to welcome its congregation.

When John Hill Martin was informed that a new Roman Catholic church had been built on the beach site and his authority and claim to the title of the site set at naught, he was furious. However, as the church was built, there was nothing he could do but wait and take a civil action for trespass in the Southern Circuit Court in the spring.

In the meantime, once the church was built, Father Duffy petitioned Martin to remove the fish flake he had built around the beach as it constituted a public nuisance to the whole community. It also blocked access to the new church. Martin refused to remove the flake and before leaving in early January to attend the winter sitting of the House of Assembly at St. John's ordered his clerks to refuse to sell Father Duffy any supplies.

On January 12, 1835, Father Duffy sent down to Slade Elson for a gallon of brandy. William Lush, the chief clerk, refused to supply it. It was the final straw for Father Duffy and the next morning, January 13, he took action. William Lush, in a sworn statement before Judge Boulton, later described the events that followed:

> . . . That about 9:00 o'clock of the morning of Friday, January 13th., in the present year this informant perceived smoke to issue from the said fish room and premises, and immediately proceeded to the same, where he found James Duffy one of the R.C. priests of this island together with Michael Christopher, alias Yetman, Pat Tobin, John Bowan, Stephen Connors, Thomas Murray, James Whelan, James Faegan the elder, John Bishop, and Geoffery Quilty and divers other persons amounting to the number of 80 or upwards, all of whom were unlawfully, riotously and tumultuously assembled to the disturbance of the public peace of St. Mary's, and did with force demolish and pull down, and burn and destroy the greater part of the flake on the before mentioned fish room. That the greater part of the people then assembled were employed in destroying

the flake, some cutting it down with hatchets while others laid it in piles and set fire to it. That this informant heard then and there, the said James Duffy, a Catholic Priest aforesaid order the persons assembled, as aforesaid to do and commit the damages and injury mentioned. That informant then approached the said James Duffy and said he had come to request the said James Duffy, and the people there assembled would desist, and the reply given to the informant was that Mr. Martin had been appraised of the intention to destroy the said flake which would be carried into effect, that the said James Duffy then assisted and directed the destruction of the said flake and ordered the people there present to persevere in their labour of destruction. That he, James Duffy seemed to take more interest in the destruction of the said flake by giving his assistance in beating it up and tossing it on the fire. That this informant spoke to several persons then assembled and requested they would desist from doing what was wrong, and some of them replied they were ordered by their priest to destroy the flake and could not leave off, and this was said by Michael Christopher otherwise known as Yetman. That the said flake was two hundred feet in length and twenty-four feet in breath . . . that said informant had heard from Philip Breen, John Tobin, Michael Adams, Michael Roache, Martin Kearney and others of the men under the command of the said James Duffy on the day aforesaid, that James Duffy had told the congregation in chapel to break up and burn the flake and that those who might refuse to do so should have the curse of God and the curse of the congregation upon them, and this informant saith that he heard Michael Roach say that James Duffy said they should burn and destroy the flake and he James Duffy would be accountable and the Devil might go with those who did not assist.

Signed: William Lush
Sworn before me the 24th., of November 1835.
H.J. Bolton, Chief Justice.[1]

---

1 *Alberti Transcripts*, C.O. i93/194, 194/194, p. 8-16.

A Second Flake Burning Incident:

On January 13, 1835, only a limited portion of Martin's flake was destroyed. A few days later Martin was again requested to remove the flake. Martin again refused to have the remainder of the flake taken down. On January 30, 1835, Father Duffy and his men finished the job of cutting down the remainder of flake.

Judge Boulton and the Supreme Court:

In the meantime John Hill Martin was advised by the Chief Justice, Henry Boulton, not to lay trespass and damages charges in the court at St. Mary's, but rather to wait and lay charges of riot and rebellion and destruction of property against Father Duffy and his congregation in the Supreme Court, where Boulton would preside. So, when the Southern Circuit court sat in St. Mary's in the spring of 1835, no charges were brought against Father Duffy or the members of his congregation. Instead Martin, who was still in St. John's, waited until after the court was finished in St. Mary's, and then laid charges of riot and rebellion and the destruction of property. To have Father Duffy taken into custody he then wrote to the Colonial Secretary in St. John's that Father Duffy was planning to leave St. Mary's to escape the consequences of a court appearance.

> St. John's
> 20th., May 1835
>
> I feel it is my duty to appraise you that it has come to my knowledge that James Duffy, the Catholic Priest, the person who destroyed the fish flake by fire at St. Mary's on the 30th of January last is on the *eve* of leaving this country—I beg leave to request that you will make this known to his Excellency , the Governor, and also the great anxiety I feel at this moment least the said Duffy should escape.

I have the Honour
to remain Sir,
Your obedient servant
To. Sect. Crowdy John Hill Martin[1]

At around the same time Chief Justice Henry Boulton arrived back in St. John's from England and immediately issued a warrant for the arrest of Father Duffy. As promised, the charge would be heard in the Supreme Court with Judge Boulton on the bench. Boulton then sent what Bishop Anthony Fleming later termed "two common catchpoles" to arrest Father Duffy. They took him into custody and made him walk to Ferryland where he appeared before the magistrates. These magistrates, according to Bishop Fleming, "could not restrain themselves from giving expression to their satisfaction at having caught a priest." He was charged and ordered to appear before the Supreme Court at St. John's for its 1835 fall sitting. Then, having given surety for his appearance in court, he was released on bail.[2]

Father Duffy returned to St. Mary's and the fishermen who had taken part in the destruction of the flake expected that they too would be arrested. However, there were no further arrests at that time. Of course, John Hill Martin had his own reasons for delaying the arrest of the men involved with Father Duffy in the attack on the flake. All these men had been supplied for the fishery by Slade Elson & Co. and it would never do for them to lose their summer fishery. So, he waited until the fishery was over and all hands had squared up to arrest the men named by Lush in his sworn statement before the magistrate.

---

1 *Incoming Correspondence* S-2-2V p. 54
2 Howley, p. 327

The Attempt to Arrest Eight men at St. Mary's:

In the fall of 1835, an attempt was made to arrest the men named in Lush's deposition. Father Duffy was absent from the community, having left St. Mary's to walk nearly one hundred miles over the trackless bogs to St. John's for the fall session of the Supreme Court. When his case came up, Judge Boulton postponed it until the 1836 spring session of the court. At the same time, Martin laid charges in the Supreme Court against Michael Christopher, otherwise known as Yetman, Patrick Tobin, Stephen Connors, Thomas Murray, Thomas Whelan, James Fagan the elder, John Bishop and Geoffery Quilty as being leaders with Father Duffy in the riot at St. Mary's and warrants were then issued for their arrest. The Attorney General of Newfoundland ordered the Captain of the Colonial Brig *Maria* to take on board two constables and sail to St. Mary's to arrest and bring back the eight fishermen named in the warrants. At first only one constable, a man named Richard Butt, was willing to go on this mission, but eventually another constable named Hurley also agreed to go.

The *Maria* arrived off St. Mary's about nine o'clock on the evening of December 15, and Captain Buoy and the two constables took certain precautions to keep their arrival unknown to the people of St. Mary's. The brig stood off shore and a boat was sent in the harbour with the mate, two constables and a sailor to contact Martin and see how he wanted them to proceed. On landing they told some of the residents that they had been cast away at Trepassey and were in need of provisions. Leaving the sailor to look after the boat, the mate and two constables then went to Martin's house to consult with him.

Martin wanted to proceed immediately and arrest the eight men named in the warrant before any resistance could be organized. To assist the two constables from St. John's and point out the residences of the men to be arrested, he sent for Mr. Burke, the local constable.

On arriving at Martin's house Constable Burke opposed Martin's plan of trying to make the arrests at night. He told Martin and the constables there would be no element of surprise as the arrival of the *Maria* had been expected and the people knew that she had arrived. He also said that the eight men named in the warrant did not mean to go without a fight, and to help each other they had arranged a signal system of showing a light in a certain window if any attempt was made by the police to arrest them. He further added that the whole harbour was agreed to join together to prevent the arrest of the eight men named in the warrant.

It was decided to wait until the next day to execute the warrants and the constables returned to their ship. The next morning Constable Burke refused to help the St. John's constables because he had been threatened with death if he lent any assistance. Martin dismissed him and ordered Butt and Hurley to come ashore and do their duty.

Later, In a sworn statement Constable Hurley described his attempt to make an arrest.

The information of William Hurley of St. John's in the Island of Newfoundland, constable. Taken before me Peter W. Carter, Esquire, one of His Majesty's Justices of the Peace for the Central District of the said Island this 28th., day of December, 1835, who said that on the thirteenth instant having arrived at St. Mary's he went on shore and visited the residence of Mr. J. H. Martin with Richard Butt and the mate of the yacht *Maria* for the purpose of showing the warrants and papers he had brought from St. John's to Mr. Martin. That Martin read the said statements then sent for William Burke who on arriving at Martin's house and being required to go with informant and Butt to the houses of some of the parties mentioned refused to do so. There were 30 or 40 armed men near the premises of Mr. Martin and they had said they would take the life of the first man who attempted to take them. That on the refusal of the said William Burke to do this duty he was dismissed by Mr. Martin from his office, that after the mob had dispersed Butt and informant went on board the yacht having been accompanied by two of Mr. Martin's men to the boat. That on the 15th instant Informant and Butt again went ashore by direction of said John Martin and met at the landing place a large collection of men who permitted them to land without issuing any obstruction. That Thomas Murray was pointed out to Informant on the same day by Mr. Martin from his window who is named in said warrant. This Informant then approached said Murray telling him he had a warrant against said Murray. Then, Michael Fagan, son of James Fagan the Elder of St. Mary, aforesaid, assaulted, and knocked this informant down and then ran under the flake for stones but was prevented from doing further injury to Informant by John Quilty. That Informant went to the house of Mr. Martin's and remained there until the mob dispersed and he heard the said Michael Fagan say they would go on board the yacht and tear her in pieces and that from the violence used by the said persons it was impossible to arrest the persons named in said warrant.

Signed: William Hurley.

The next two days, Thursday and Friday, it blew a gale and there was no communications between the *Maria* and the shore. On Saturday, Martin sent a note to Captain Buoy saying that as the constables could not arrest the persons named in the warrant, they should address a public notice to the parties concerned, calling on them to surrender in the king's name. Captain Buoy later described what happened when he attempted to serve a summons:

> The information of William W. Buoy of St. John's, Master of the Colonial Yacht *Maria*, taken before me Peter W. Carter on the 28th day of December, 1835 who says that on the

14th., he went to the house of Michael Roach, to whom informant said, "I have come to serve you with a subpoena to go to St. John's and give evidence against James Duffy—that Roach replied he would have nothing to do with it and deponent then laid the said subpoena close to the foot of the said Roach, who stood in the chimney corner, and laid a shilling upon it, telling at the same time the said Roach that he need not be afraid of the subpoena as it was only to make a witness of him. That Roach then took up a gun and raising the butt about two feet high placed it on a form and told informant "to be off from his house." Then, informant said if you can't read the sub-poena I will do it for you, as I wish to give you good advice. That thereupon the said Roach lifted the gun and shook it in such a manner that alarmed the informant who then left the house. That a little girl followed informant to the corner of the house and threw the subpoena and shilling at informant's feet who left them both there. The said house was pointed out by a servant in the employment of Mr. Martin and informant required him to note what had passed, to which he replied, "I will be no witness."

Signed: W.H. Buoy
Sworn before me 28th December, 1835
Peter W. Carter (Magistrate)[1]

As it now seemed impossible to make any arrests or even serve subpoenas and warrants the *Maria* returned to St. John's and reported the failure of their mission. Father Duffy had not returned from his trek to St. John's when the attempt to make the arrests had been made, but arrived footsore and weary a few days later. On his return he was greeted with the new developments that had taken place. However, as winter had now set in it was unlikely that any further action would be taken until the spring, so the people of St. Mary's settled

---

1   Ibid

down to enjoy the Christmas season, and wait for further government action.

Before the colonial yacht *Maria* left St. Mary's, John Hill Martin gave Captain Buoy a letter to be delivered to the Colonial Secretary giving his own personal account of the events following the arrival of the colonial yacht on December 13th, 1835. He ended with a request for enforcement of the law at St. Mary's:

> . . . Any observations coming from me in reference to the foregoing narrative many be termed presumptuous but I cannot allow the opportunity to pass without requesting you to express to His Excellency, the governor, my regret that it should have fallen to my lot to reside among persons who should raise up an army against their sovereign and the law of our country. I do indulge in the hope that such outrageous conduct may not be suffered to pass by with impunity, not only for the sake of punishing past delinquency but to prevent the reoccurrence of future crime.
>
> I have the Honour to remain
> Your Obedient Servant
> To Sect. Crowdy: John Hill Martin.[1]
> December 22, 1835.

The colonial yacht arrived back in St. John's and Martin's letter was delivered by Secretary Crowdy to Governor Prescott. The governor thought the matter serious enough to write the Rt. Honourable Lord Glenly at the Colonial Office in London giving some background information on St. Mary's and including copies of Martin's letter of December 22, 1835 and Lush's sworn statement about the events at St. Mary's. He asked for a ship and men to enforce the law there.

---

1 *Local Correspondence*, S2,19, pp. 10-16

Your Lordship having informed me that the Colonial Vessel is to be discontinued, it being certain the legislature will not support her, I shall have no means of sending a military detachment to St. Mary's on this occasion, indeed the presence of a ship of war is more desirable, and my idea is a small frigate should arrive in St. John's in the latter part of April exclusively devoted to this service and independent of any force destined for the usual protection of the fishery. Here she will receive on board 20 or 30 men of the Veseron Corps, an intelligent magistrate and law officer and trustworthy constables, and proceed to St. Mary's.

I trust that such a demonstration accompanied by a proclamation may induce the offenders and required witnesses to come forward and yield to the law. If on the contrary they should abandon their homes and families and go into the interior, the ship and troops must remain. The latter can be perfectly accommodated in a large empty house belonging to Mr. Martin and provisions are abundant,

The stay of the frigate must of course be regulated by weather and other circumstances.

I hope your lordship will approve of this arrangement and procure a ship of war to be sent here in accordance with it.

Your Humble etc.
H. Prescott.[1]

The Threat of Occupation:

On February 5th, 1836, Lord Glenely replied to Governor Prescott that he was in full agreement that such disregard for the authority of the king must be punished, and promised to send the requested warship in the spring. However, he did point out that any threatened resistance to the law should be handled in such a way as would permit the least possible

---

1 *Alberti Transcripts*,C.O 194/94, 1836 p. 1-5

hazard to the person and property of His Majesty's subjects. On February 18, 1836 he advised Governor Prescott that Vice-Admiral, Sir George Copburn was sending a vessel to assist the governor in putting down the rebellion at St. Mary's.

After the departure of the Colonial Yacht and the constables, St. Mary's settled down for the winter. Then rumours began to circulate that in the spring a British warship would arrive bringing troops to occupy St. Mary's and bring those charged in the destruction of the flake to justice. On May 7, 1836 Governor Prescott issued a Royal Proclamation calling on all the persons concerned in the affair to surrender themselves to the civil process of the law. The Royal Proclamation appeared in the May 10th editions of both *The Royal Gazette* and *Newfoundland Advertiser*. and was also posted in St. Mary's.[1] It struck a chill in the hearts of all the people, as it was expected that the war ship with the British troops would soon arrive. Still the men named in the warrants resisted the idea of giving themselves up without a fight. Then Michael Anthony Fleming, the Roman Catholic bishop at St. John's, took a hand in the proceedings.

Bishop Fleming's Pastoral Letter:

On hearing that Governor Prescott had issued a Royal Proclamation on May 7, 1836, calling on the men of St. Mary's to surrender, and that a British frigate and troops were to be soon sent to St. Mary's, Bishop Fleming became fearful. He was afraid that such an incident would reflect poorly on all the Irish Roman Catholics, lessen their political influence and perhaps result in the loss of the Newfoundland Legislature. To encourage the men named in the 1835 November warrant to come to St. John's and give themselves up, he sent a pastoral letter dated May 10, 1836, to be read at all masses in

---

1   See Appendix for text of Proclamation

St. Mary's, painting a grim picture of the results of an occupation by British troops. Father Duffy read the letter as directed by his bishop.

The Pastoral Letter:
The letter began:

To Our Beloved Children in Christ Jesus, The People of St. Mary's Bay

Beloved Children:
With a bosom burning with affection and a heart agitated with anxious cares and solicitude for your spiritual and temporal welfare, it becomes our painful duty to address you on a subject as important to your eternal happiness as to your worldly peace.

Man's duties here on earth may be classed into political and personal duties, and it is the great object of religion to enforce their fulfilment, and upon the manner in which and the motive with which both are discharged will depend our future misery or eternal bliss.

Bishop Fleming then outlined the course of events leading up to the arrival of Constables Butt and Hurley to arrest the men named by Lush. He then warned them that they were judged as being in a state of rebellion and that two warships were to be sent to blocade their harbour and a garrison of soldiers was to be quartered upon them. In very graphic terms he outlined the possible consequences if the men named in the warrants did not go to St. John's and give themselves up.

Some people my Beloved Children laugh at the silly notion of sending a blockading squadron to St. Mary's Bay on so foolish an errand. It may be amusing to some but to us it brings naught but affliction of the spirit. For who can contemplate the establishment of a military Section among your wives and daughters at a season when of necessity your avocations will require the abandonment of your families, of your homes and firesides to the unbridled licentiousness of soldiers without the presence of a single magistrate, a single local tribunal to restrain them.

How then are you to prevent this violent outrage being perpetrated in the names of the laws? Let every man of the following persons whose names are mentioned in the Proclamation viz: Michael Christopher, Pat Tobin, Stephen Connors, Thomas Murray, Thomas Whelan, James Fagan the Elder, John Bishop, and Geoffery Quilty, come forward to St. John's and tender bail for their appearances. This will be the means of proving to those evilly disposed characters that no circumstances or irritation will or can seduce you into a violation of the law.

Beloved Children of Christ have no apprehension in surrendering yourselves to the award of the law. It is only the guilty that need fear punishment and even if the innocent should from any motive be made the victims of persecution their causes must eventually triumph and Justice be proudly vindicated.

There stands at the helm of the Government of your Island a man, whom, in my heart I believe to be determined to relieve the oppressed, to vindicate the injured and although perhaps the *only* man in office in this country who is not *directly* opposed to the principles of His Majesty's Government—standing alone against a host—yet that man vested as he is with vice-regal power equitably fulfilling the great object of his mission to Newfoundland will be your refuge and protection from the evil machinations of the true disturbers of the peace.

+ Michael Anthony Fleming
Bishop of Carpasia
Vicar—Apolostic of Newfoundland.
St. John,s, May 10, 1836.[1]

---

1 *Alberti Transcripts*, 1836

Bishop Fleming's Pastoral Letter may have raised some doubts in the minds of the St. Mary's people concerning his definition of their political responsibilities, but there were none concerning the duty of the men named in the Proclamation. The bishop had been very explicit about what would happen to the women of St. Mary's when the British troops arrived, and made it clear that this could only be avoided by their going to St. John's and surrendering to the courts. The men named in the proclamation had no choice for they could no longer count on the support of their neighbours. There was only one consolation: Bishop Fleming had made it possible for them to give themselves up gracefully by telling them to put their fate in Governor Prescott's sense of justice.

The next day, May 11, the eight men made ready for the long hard journey over the bogs and marshes to St. John's. Father Duffy, who also had to make the trip again, accompanied them. As soon as they left the community, John Hill Martin wrote the governor that in obedience to their bishop's request, the men named in the Proclamation had left St. Mary's for St. John's. They had been told that they must be in St. John's before June 22, or a warship would sail on that day for St. Mary's:

The Origin of Father Duffy's Well

Father Duffy and his companions left St. Mary's before daylight and by nightfall they had reached a spot on what is now the Salmonier Line about mid-way between St. Mary's and St. John's. It was also part of an old trail that led from Renews on the Southern Shore to St. Mary's. Here they decided to camp for the night. The men were tired and thirsty and very low in spirits. When they could find no water to fill their kettle to make tea, they became very dejected and it was then Father Duffy performed what his companions came to believe was a miracle.

He didn't say anything to them, but he took a small stick in his hand, went up to a large rock and dug a small hole at its base. He tapped the rock gently with the stick, and to the amazement of his companions a trickle of water appeared and in a few minutes the hole was full and overflowing. The St. Mary's men were filled with awe. Surely this must be a miracle. They filled their kettle, boiled up, and then lay down to rest, confident that no harm could come to them with such a man as their leader. From that very time Father Duffy's well on the Salmonier Line has always been regarded by many people as a holy well with curative powers.

Victory at Last:

It was early May when Father Duffy and his companions reached St. John's and the seven men from St. Mary's surrendered to the court. They were charged and bound over to appear at the next sitting of the Supreme Court which was set for mid-July, 1836. This was a very serious blow to the fishermen from St. Mary's for they could lose the caplin scull fishery. The fishermen then petitioned the governor setting out their defence of their actions and asking that the trial date be changed so as not to endanger the fishery.[1]

Following their petition to the governor, the men of St. Mary's were successful in getting the trial date changed to December, 1836. Father Duffy's trial was also moved up to December as no witnesses from the prosecution had turned up to testify against him. In December, 1836, Father Duffy and the men from St. Mary's again travelled to St. John's for trial. They went to court and the indictment against them was read.[2]

However as no witnesses for the prosecution turned up, the trial was again postponed until the spring of 1837.

---

1   See Appendix
2   See Appendix for text of Indictment.

In the spring of 1837, Father Duffy and his companions again travelled to St. John's for their court appearance. Once again no witness for the prosecution came forward, but this time on orders from Governor Prescott the trial went ahead. The prisoners pleaded not guilty and with no witnesses for the prosecution the charges against Father Duffy and the St. Mary's men were stayed. This ended the case, but for several years afterwards Roman Catholic politicians in St. John's used the Duffy case as a prime example of the abuses of Chief Justice Henry Boulton as a judge, and the case helped in having him removed from office.

Father Duffy remained at St. Mary's until 1841 when he left Newfoundland and accepted a parish in Nova Scotia. He later went to the parish of King's Cross in Prince Edward Island where he died in 1859.

*Father Duffy's Monument at King's Cross,
Prince Edward Island*

Courtesy of Mr. Edgar Blundon

Carbonear

Chapter Fourteen

Politics and The Assaults on Henry Winton and Herman Lott

The Assault on Henry Winton:

Following the first general election in Newfoundland in 1832, and Bishop Fleming's successful entry into the political arena in defence of John Kent, the Newfoundland Irish led by their Roman Catholic clergy became a very important political factor in Newfoundland politics. Besides Bishop Fleming, there was Father E. Troy who didn't hesitate to use the power of the priesthood to intimidate and bring to heel anyone who dared to oppose the political candidates supported by the Roman Catholic Church. In 1834, Timothy Hogan had been forced by undue clerical pressure to resign from contesting a St. John's seat in opposition to Dr. William Carson. In May of 1835, Henry Winton, who had opposed the election of Kent and then attacked all things Irish and Roman Catholic in his paper, *The Public Ledger*, was the victim of a brutal assault on Saddle Hill between Carbonear and Harbour Grace. Though it was never proven, the assault was blamed on the Irish of the area.

The Attack on Saddle Hill:

On May 19, 1835, Henry Winton on horseback and Captain Churchward of the brig *Hazard* on foot, were returning to Harbour Grace from Carbonear at around 4:00 p.m.,

> when a gang of ruffians hideously disguised with painted faces suddenly issued from the woods on the right of the road. Instantly the foremost of them with uplifted arm, approached Mr. Winton, and by a heavy blow on the side of the head, with one of the stones, felled him from his horse, whilst others sprang towards Capt. Churchward and effectually prevented him from rendering any assistance.

Captain Churchward was rendered helpless by several heavy blows to the head and then taken into the woods and threatened with death if he called out. *The Public Ledger* described the vicious assault on Henry Winton:

> The savages, however, had not completed their diabolic purpose. Not content with the brutal violence they had committed upon the victim they proceeded to fill his ears with mud and gravel—and to the question, "Do you mean to murder me?" one of the ruffians replied, "Hold your tongue, you —, and then opening a clasp knife stooped down and mutilated one of the ears. At this period one of the gang exclaimed, "Hold his hands," whilst another called out, "Here he is—we have him." they then took off the other ear, and left their victim insensible. Upon recovering, which Mr. Winton thinks must have been shortly afterwards, he found himself alone and bleeding.[1]

Captain Churchward came to Winton's assistance and they made their way to Dr. Stirling in Harbour Grace who stopped the bleeding and skilfully stitched the wounds.

The attack on Winton served to widen the gap between

---

1   *The Public Ledger*, June 2, 1835

the Roman Catholic Irish and the English Protestants. Though never proved, it was suspected that the attack was made by Irish Roman Catholics in retaliation for the disparaging articles Winton had written on the Irish Roman Catholic Clergy and especially one about the Presentation Sisters. However, despite a reward of 500 pounds posted by the governor and 1,000 pounds by the St. John's merchants, the attackers were never brought to justice.

Henry Winton recovered and continued his war of words against Dr. Carson, Bishop Fleming and the Roman Catholic clergy. Strangely enough, some years later, Henry Winton's wife reported that Bishop Fleming made his way to Winton's house and asked to see Winton. He told Winton's wife his days were numbered and he wanted to die at peace with his neighbours. The two men had a long private conversation and peace was restored. Later they were even seen walking together on the most friendly terms.[1]

Trouble at the Harbour Grace Election:

The Newfoundland election of 1836 resulted in a large Irish Roman Catholic majority. With the exception of Dr. Carson, who had the full approval of the Roman Catholic clergy, and four mercantile candidates, all the members elected were Roman Catholics. This was brought about by a solid Roman Catholic vote in the districts which had a majority of Roman Catholics and by intimidation and physical violence in the larger centres. For example in Harbour Grace, the first voters to attempt to vote for the mercantile candidate were severely beaten and his other supporters were too afraid to come forward to vote. The church approved candidate was supported from the pulpit and his opponent condemned by the Roman Catholic priests. After several days of violence in the

---

1   Pedley, p. 387

streets, the mercantile candidate withdrew from the contest and the other won by default.

[1] Then came a problem. Judge Boulton pointed out that the election writs issued for the election of 1836 did not bear the Great Seal and were thus invalid. As a result, the election was declared invalid and a new election was held in June 1837. Once again the Catholics won all but 4 seats, and formed the government. Among those elected were E. J. Dwyer of Lions Den, Fogo. Rumour had it that his supplier was to get one half of his sessional pay. Trinity returned Thomas Fitzgerald Moore, a rather eccentric character, a country guide, who carried a "nunny" bag on a stick over his shoulders on his way to the House of Assembly. According to Governor Prescott the main aim of the elected members was "the reward of friends and the punishment of foes." One thing was now certain, the Irish Roman Catholic of Newfoundland controlled the Newfoundland House of Assembly. However, some Irish Newfoundland Roman Catholics opposed the Church's direct involvement in politics. As Mr. (Sir) Richard Bonneycastle observed in a report to the British Colonial Office, politically the Roman Catholics in Newfoundland were divided between the "Mad Dogs" or independents Irish Roman Catholics, and the "Priests' Party" who looked to Bishop Fleming for guidance. However he also defended Bishops Fleming saying that although he was "ambitious and bigoted" he had nevertheless publicly been greatly maligned by the merchants and government officials in a local newspaper.[2]

The Removal of Chief Justice Boulton:

In 1838, the struggle to remove Judge Boulton as Chief Justice intensified and the Newfoundland Legislature sent a

---

1   CO 194/95 Governor Prescott to Lord Glenelg, December 9, 1836.
2   Gunn, Gertrude, *The Political History of Newfoundland*, p. 81.

delegation to London to press the Colonial Office for his removal. A petition with thousands of signatures demanding the removal of Judge Boulton was forwarded to the king. The Privy Council studied the charges against Boulton, but found that no corrupt motive could be attributed to any of his judicial decisions. Despite this finding however, they recommended that he be removed from the Newfoundland court. When news of this reached Newfoundland there was great rejoicing and his enemies gave their own interpretation of the decision of the Privy Council to remove Boulton.

Huzza, huzza, huzza !!!

Fishermen rejoice! There is some hope for you, that the wages for which you have toiled and perilled your lives will not again be snatched from you by the edicts of an unjust and despotic judge! Current supplies—let your joy animate your bosoms! the law broken to injure you, and set aside for the vilest party purposes, will again become your security.

Victims of judicial tyranny, persecuted priests and people! all Newfoundland, lift up your hearts in thankfulness to God! Boulton is convicted! condemned! Sentenced![1]

With the removal of Judge Boulton one of the causes of the political unrest in Newfoundland was removed, and the way paved for less partisan violence at the polls. Intervention from Rome would also eventually reduce direct political activity of the Roman Catholic clergy.

An Appeal to Rome:

As early as 1834, the British Colonial Office forwarded through a British agent in Rome, an appeal to the Vatican to curb the involvement of Bishop Fleming and his Irish born

---

1 Pedley p. 402

clergy in Newfoundland politics. The Vatican Secretary of State, Cardinal Bernetti, promised to convey to Bishop Fleming the Pope's disapproval of his political activity, but Cardinal Bernetti fell ill and the matter was forgotten. Some time later Cardinal Capaccini, Bernetti's successor, promised to send a letter to Bishop Fleming on the matter. Fleming answered the letter and said his enemies, both Roman Catholic and Protestant, were "dangerous innovators." The Vatican took no further action and Bishop Fleming and his clergy reamined active in the political life of the colony.[1]

In 1837, Governor Prescott was ordered by the British Colonial Secretary to prepare a dossier on Bishop Fleming and his partisan involvement in Newfoundland politics. Bishop Fleming was in England when the dossier was compiled, but on returning home and learning about the investigation, returned immediately to London to defend himself. The information collected was sent through the British Foreign Office to Rome. The British Agent in Rome made sure it came to the attention of the Pope. The report included accounts of the actions of Father Troy during Bishop Fleming's absence, of frequent denials of religious rites and physical expulsion from the chapel. One such case was that of Michael Scanlan.

The Persecution of Michael Scanlan:

Michael Scanlan, a St. John's shop keeper, had served for a number of years as clerk of the R.C. Chapel during the episcopate of Bishop Scallan. His story illustrates what could happen even to a respectable Roman Catholic of independent mind: "A Mad Dog" to the Priest's Party.

On the 26th of November 1836, Scanlan swore out a complaint before Magistrate Carter of ill-treatment received when he went with his family to attend mass at the old chapel.

_____

1 CO 194/92, W.F. Strangeways to Hay, October 25, 1835.

The complaint and information of Michael Scanlan of St. John's, dealer, who saith that on Sunday the 13th of this instant on the morning of that day between the hours of 9:00 and 10:00 o'clock repaired to R.C. chapel in company with his wife Eleanor and Mary Scanlan his daughter for the purpose of performing their religious duties. That shortly having entered the pew the Reverend E. Troy ascended the altar and said, "I saw Thomas Grace and Michael Scanlan coming here, they must leave the chapel immediately, as I cannot say mass while they are present," and afterwards said, "Are they gone? are they going?"

Deponent then rose in his pew and begged of the Reverend Father Troy to state to the congregation what deponent had done amiss and repeated his words twice. The Reverend Father Troy made no reply but took off his vestments and rushed through the congregation to the stairs of that part of the chapel where deponent's pew is situated. That Peter Broaders of St. John's, labourer and others standing in the passage near deponent's pew who cried out together for the deponent to be off. Upon which some person seized him by the collar of his coat saying, "You must be off." That deponent thought resistance was in vain and went out, but looked back and saw Broaders lay hold of his wife saying, "his strumpet of a wife must be off after him." That deponent received a kick on the stairs going down and was dragged out of the chapel when John O'Mara of St. John's, dealer, laid hold of deponent saying "you must be off," forcing him away. That deponent then addressed the people outside and said he was cruelly used, that he had a wife and family and had resided in St. John's for 21 years and considered himself as good a Roman Catholic as any present. That the said O'Mara with both his hands violently pushed deponent upon a small heap of stones, that deponent got up when a multitude of people were around him, some of whom were threatening him with obstruction whilst others were endeavouring to assist deponent and pacify the crowd. That afterwards the said John O'Mara took hold of deponent and pushed him along

saying " you must not remain here exciting the people. That Father Berrigan came out of the Bishop's house and protected deponent as far as the lane when he returned to his own house and his daughter and wife returned about half-an-hour afterwards.
Signed: Michael Scanlan[1]

Mrs. Scanlan confirmed under oath her husband's story but added that after Broaders had pushed her towards the stairs calling her "a strumpet," he took hold of her daughter Mary, gave her a violent shove so that she fell down in the pew and said,"This faggot of a daughter must be off after them." Her daughter cried and seemed about to faint when Mr. John Shea and others came to her assistance. However, the magistrate noted that Mrs. Scanlan would not confirm or deny the words used by Father Troy.

Refusal of Last Rites To Lawrence Barron:

Lawrence Barron of St John's was another Roman Catholic whose political views opposed those of Father Troy. As a result he was refused the last rites. Barron being very ill, his wife sent two neighbours to the priest's house to get the priest to come to render the last rites. Father Waldron agreed to go and prepare the man for death. Father Troy, who had been left in charge by Bishop Fleming, prevented Father Waldron from going. Troy said that no priest should prepare him, and that was the way in which all "Mad Dogs" should die. He went on to say that not one of them would be alive in five years. He also threatened that if Father Waldron or any other priest went, he would have the vestments off them. Later a Mr. Moasey came to Barron's house and said if Barron would sign an apology to the clergy they would come. Barron refused and later received a letter for him to sign, but he

---

1   GN5/2/A/1 (8) p. 89

refused again. He died without the priest and Troy would not let any of the Roman Catholic priests attend his burial service.[1]

Meanwhile the British agent at Rome was able to report back to the Foreign Office that after the dispatch from the Foreign Office, the Pope had ordered the Propaganda to despatch letters ordering the Bishop to suspend immediately any priest who intervened in political affairs. The Bishop too had been rebuked for allowing such activities. At this time Bishop Fleming was in London and unaware of the manoeuvring in Rome. He complained about the dossier compiled on his activities, but was assured by the British Authorities that no action would be taken against him on the basis of the Governor's dossier. He also obtained the piece of land he needed to build a new cathedral, and, anxious to get started on his long cherished project, agreed that it was time to restore harmony in Newfoundland.

On his return to Newfoundland Bishop Fleming received the letters from Rome and took immediate steps to follow the orders from the Vatican. He published a letter exhorting all Roman Catholics to forgive their enemies and make them their friends. He also transferred Father Edward Troy to a newly created parish on the Island of Merasheen in Placentia Bay which allowed him to stay in Newfoundland, but effectively curtailed his further involvement in political activities.[2]

However, Bishop Fleming's silence on political matters was short lived. In 1840, he and his clergy again became involved in by-elections at St. John's and Carbonear.

Clerical Involvement In The St. John's By-Election:

The St. John's by-election was called for May, and James Douglas, a Scots Presbyterian who had the full support of

---

1 Ibid.
2 *Patriot* October 27, 1838, Bishop Fleming's Letter.

both Protestants and Roman Catholics, was nominated to contest the election. Then, after nearly three years of silence on political matters, Bishop Fleming again became involved. At the last moment, he ordered a Roman Catholic candidate, Lawrence O'Brien, to run against Douglas. Douglas had been nominated by Lawrence O'Brien, but when Bishop Fleming ordered O'Brien to run he became a rival candidate. Three days before the election one of the priests read a letter from the pulpit telling the congregation to vote for O'Brien. O'Brien went to political rallies accompanied by three priests.[1] A description of the election day clerical support for Mr. O'Brien has been preserved by Mr. James Murphy

> At ten o'clock the popular candidate (Mr. Douglas) took his place surrounded by his friends. Shortly afterwards O'Brien came forward supported by Fathers Waldron, Walsh and Forrestal and Messrs Nugent and Kent, and erected his flag. O'Brien himself was trimmed with green and carried a green banner in his hand, his followers also wearing green badges. The popular candidate had nothing, nor his friends to distinguish them beyond their respectable appearance. By agreement between the candidates, four individuals of each party was deputed to stand at the polling table to examine the qualifications of each voter. Mr. Douglas's four were, Mr. Walsh, Mr. Duggan, Mr. Brien, and Mr. Barron. Mr. O'Brien's were Fr. Walsh, Fr. Waldreon, John V. Nugent and John Kent.[2]

There had been faction fights and much disorder before polling day. The priests were said to have used horse whips to quell opposition to their candidate. Governor Prescott even accused the priests of being in the polling room threatening spiritual punishments on any Roman Catholic who

---

1   CO 194/109, Governor Prescott to Lord Russell, June 10, 1840.
2   Murphy James, *Customs of the Past*, p.7

voted against O'Brien. When the polling was finished O'Brien was the winner.[1]

The Midnight Questioning of Herman Lott.

On February 14, 1840. Mr. Herman Lott, the foreman of the *Public Ledger* had a strange and rather terrifying experience. He was going home around midnight when he was seized from behind and his eyes bandaged. He was then led to a house some distance away and placed in a room. The bandage was removed and he found himself in a room hung with white cloth, with even the ceiling covered. Seated by a blazing fireplace were two masked and hooded figures all dressed in black. They interrogated Mr. Lott, asking him such questions as whether Henry Winton had arms in his house, or carried arms when he went abroad. They also wanted the names of the people who wrote for the paper. At the end of the interrogation, Mr. Lott was warned to keep silent about what had happened and threatened with punishment if he spoke about the affair. Then his eyes were again bandaged and he was taken back to the place where he had been seized and let go. By the time he had the bandages off his eyes his enemies had vanished.

Mr. Lott did not keep quiet about the affair. He went and gave his story under oath before a magistrate. Three months later while travelling from Carbonear to Harbour Grace, he too was attacked on Saddle Hill, and his two ears were cut off. Again the offer of a large reward did not lead to the discovery of the culprits.[2]

Election Day Violence at Carbonear:

The by-election at Carbonear was called for December. The contest here was between two opposing Irish factions in the

---

1   Ibid.
2   Pedley, p. 397

town. One group supported Edward Hanrahan, the Bishop's candidate. Another group made up of the more independent Irish Catholics ("Mad Dogs") supported James Pendergast. On election day the mob attacked the house of Mr. Ash. He fired on the attackers and wounded five or six of them. They then set fire to his house and burnt it to the ground. Another house was torn in pieces. In the melee, a lot of other property damage also occurred. As well, Mr. Ridley, a merchant-magistrate, suffered a skull fracture when hit on the head with a picket, another person was shot in the hip, and six others had bullet wounds. The Returning Officer had to close the poll and later soldiers were sent to Carbonear to restore order. The governor felt that it was the Roman Catholic clergy who were responsible for the disturbance, even though they tried to limit the violence once it had started.[1]

The governor sent 100 soldiers to restore order, and the British Government suggested that Carbonear should no longer be a polling place. One of the leaders of the mob at Carbonear was an old man named Farrell. He later complained that "after all the murdering and blackguarding he had done in those elections, he had no berth, whilst the man he put in had "a fat office, and aiting and drinking the best in the land."[2]

A Successful Appeal to Rome:

The active involvement of Bishop Fleming and his clergy in the by-elections forced the British Government to again appeal to Rome. They forwarded the information gathered on Bishop Fleming by Governor Prescott to Rome.[3] This time the Pope ordered Bishop Fleming to come to Rome to answer to the charges against him. What transpired between

---

1 CO 194/109 Governor Prescott to Lord Russell.
2 Prowse, (1895) p. 438
3 Howley, p. 265.

the Pope and Bishop Fleming has never been revealed, but
with the support of the Irish members of the Francisan Order
he remained as Bishop of Newfoundland. However, from
1841 until his death in 1850 he never again became involved
in elections, but devoted his energies to providing educational opportunities for his people and building a cathedral
at St. John's.

Bishop Michael Anthony Fleming

Old Orphan Asylum School before 1840

Chapter Fifteen

Education for the Newfoundland-Irish

First Irish Schools:

Educational opportunity for the children of Irish Roman Catholics in Newfoundland was first provided by itinerant Irish school masters who operated private schools in St. John's and some of the outlying settlements. At St. John's there is a report of a papist school in existence in 1744, but nothing else is known about it.[1] Some of the early Irish school masters in the St. John's area were: Jeremiah McCarthy, Michael Howlett and Richard Coyle. Alexander O'Donovan, a professor from Cork, was a great educator at the Carbonear Grammar School during the first half of the 19th century.

At Renews, the first Irish schoolmaster was a Mr. O'Neill. He opened his school around 1815, and was retained when the goverment school was established in the community. His students called him "Old Tack" behind his back, and his harsh discipline was legendary in the community. He taught in Renews until about 1871.

---

1 Rowe, F.W., *The History of Education in Newfoundland*, p. 27.

In 1805, James MacBraire, who operated a branch of his business at King's Cove, Bonavista Bay, hired Thomas Walsh, an Irish planter of that community, to conduct a school for all the children of the community. Walsh also kept a night school for adults. When the first government Commercial or high school opened in King's Cove, another Irishman, Michael Cuddihy, was the teacher.

The first official school dedicated to the teaching of both Roman Catholic and Protestant Irish children was provided by the Benevolent Irish Society. In 1826 classes began in the house of a Mister Gill with Mr. Henry Simms as teacher. In the summer of 1827 the students moved to the classrooms provided in the new Orphan Asylum building. The school had an enrollment of between 400-500 Irish-Newfoundland students and was co-educational until 1833, when a separate Roman Catholic girls' school was established.

Bishop Fleming Takes Control of the Orphan Asylum School:

One of the first acts of Bishop Fleming after his consecration as bishop was to assert his authority over the Orphan Asylum school. This school, which was set up in 1826 by the Benevolent Irish Society, was non-denominational and the society jealously guarded its non denominational character. Even when the student body became one hundred percent Roman Catholic, they would not permit any religious instructions in the school. Bishop Fleming, while still a priest, went to the school to give religious instructions and was refused permission by the school committee. When he became bishop he insisted on giving religious instructions after school and the committee gave in. Some 400 children were prepared for communion and Bishop Fleming was able to boast that: "from that time forward the school has been placed under my immediate supervision."[1]

---

1 *Centenary Volume, Benevolent Irish Society*, 1906, p. 76.

The Establishment of the Presentation Sisters School:

Bishop Fleming felt that boys and girls needed different types of education, and he persuaded the Sisters of the Presentation Order from Ireland establish a convent and school for Roman Catholic girls in St. John's in 1833. The Presentation Convent School was very successful and before the end of the 19th century Convent Schools were established at Harbour Grace, Witless Bay, Placentia, St. Mary's, Harbour Breton and St. Jacques.

In 1842, the Sisters Of Mercy established a convent in St. John's and in 1843 opened a school for the female children of the more affluent residents of St. John's. After a few years they established convent schools at Burin, Brigus, Bay Bulls and Conception Harbour. In 1856, Bishop Mullock established an orphanage and school for Roman Catholic girls in St. John's. This establishment was operated by the Sisters of Mercy.

The Arrival of the Franciscan Monks:

Following the establishment of the Presentation and Mercy sisters in Newfoundland, the executive of the B.I.S. approached Bishop Fleming with a request that he help them find a suitable male teaching religious order to run the Orphan Asylum School. In 1847, Bishop Fleming was successful in recruiting the services of three Franciscan monks from Ireland who agreed to take over the Orphan Asylum School. The monks entered into an agreement with the B.I.S. that the society would pay their salaries and build them a monastery. Until the monastery could be built, the monks lived in a rented house near the school.

The B.I.S. expected that the arrival of the monks would see a sharp increase in the school population, and to accomodate the expected increase they spent 570 pounds enlarging and repairing the their school building. Three monks arrived in St. John's on September 7, 1847 on the steamer *Unicorn*.

Under their superior, Brother John Hanlon, they took over the residence formerly occupied by the lay teacher, Mr. Grace, and began teaching in the Orphan Asylum School.

At first, the Monks and Bishop Fleming got on well together, but soon iritations arose. In the fall of 1849, the B.I.S. rented their lecture room to a Mr. Mooney, to give a series of six lectures on the history of Ireland. After the first lecture, Bishop Fleming took exception to the material used, especially the songs, and ordered the monks to close the lecture room and forbid Mr. Mooney access. He did this without consulting the B.I.S. executive and they took exception to the Bishop's actions. The monks were caught in the middle of the row. There had already been strong differences of opinion between Brother Hanlon and Bishop Fleming and after this Brother Hanlon and Brother Bernadine returned to Ireland. Brother Angulus remained as superior and two lay teachers, Mr. Patrick Flannery and Mr. John Roche were hired to staff the school.

In 1853 Brother Angelus and his two lay teachers fell out and Brother Angelus demanded that the two lay teachers be dismissed. This was done and with the aid of a Brother Francis Grace, the school carried on. However, the parents of the students were not happy with this arrangement and by 1854 only one monk, Brother Francis Grace, remained in the colony; the remaining Franciscan monk returned to Ireland and Mr. Henry Simms, the first teacher, was again placed in charge of the Orphan Asylum school.

Later in 1854, the B.I.S. secured the services of an Irish schoolmaster, Mr. Thomas McGrath, and the school was divided into a senior and junior section. Brother Francis Grace taught the junior pupils, and Mr. McGrath and Mr. Simms taught the more advanced boys. The school continued to be conducted by lay teachers for the next twenty years. In times of plenty, the population of the school increased, but a bad fishing season forced many of the parents to keep their children home. The school continued under this system until it was taken over by the Irish Christian Brothers in 1876.

First Education Act:

In 1836, the Newfoundland Government established a non-denominational school system, but because the English Protestants and the Irish Roman Catholics could not agree on an acceptable version of the Bible for school readings, separate school systems were set up for Protestants and Roman Catholics in 1843.

In all the outlying Roman Catholic parishes the parish priests, most of whom were Irish, were the leaders in establishing schools in the community. In Witless Bay it was Dean Cleary, in Burin, Father Berney and at Tilting, Father Ward, and although small and simple affairs these schools did provide an opportunity for the children to learn to read and write and do simple calculations.

Irish Influence On Newfoundland Education:

The early Irish school masters and later the arrival of the Presentation and Mercy Sisters from Ireland did much to preserve the ties that the Newfoundland-Irish had with their mother country. The curriculum in Roman Catholic schools was based on the Irish model and the text books were similar to those used in Roman Catholic schools in Ireland. As many outport Roman Catholic teachers trained under the Sisters and later the Christian Brothers, the Irish influence was spread to the outlying harbours and did much to preserve the Irish heritage of the old country.

In 1856, Bishop Mullock established St. Bonaventure's College, a place of higher learning where boys interested in joining the priesthood could be educated. St. Bonaventure's began as a dioceesan college in a few rooms in the old palace on Henry Street, then as the number of students increase it was moved to Belvedere monastery. On April 27, 1857

Bishop Mullock laid the corner stone for a new Roman Catholic College for boys. It opened that fall for day students and the next year boarding students were accepted. In 1870 the first secular students were admitted to the college.

The first principal of St. Bon's was not an Irishman but an Italian priest, the Rt. Rev. Dr. Carfagnini, who later became bishop of Harbour Grace. However, Apart from Dr. Carfagnini the rest of the staff were Irish or Newfoundland-Irish.

The Arrival of the Irish Christian Brothers:

In the fall of 1875, Bishop Power was successful in obtaining the services of the Irish Christian Brothers. The lay teaching staff of the Orphan Asylum School was dismissed and on January 31, 1876 four Irish Christian Brothers took over and the school, which had an enrollment of 300 students. In 1880, the B.I.S. built a new school which was called St. Patrick's Hall School.

In 1889, the Irish Christian Brothers took over the administration of St. Bonaventure's College, and in 1890, established Holy Cross school in the West End of St. John's. In 1898, the order took over the Roman Catholic boys' orphanage of Mount Cashel. The order was now responsible for the education of all Roman Catholic males in St. John's.

St. Bride's College, Littledale:

In 1884, Bishop Power acquired the estate of Judge Philip Little, the first Prime Minister under Responsible Government. He opened a private boarding and day school for young Ladies. This academy, which became known as St. Bride's College or "Littledale," was operated by the Sisters of Mercy.

Villa Nova:

In 1886, Father Michael Morris, the parish priest of the parish of Topsail, opened an orphanage and school at Villa Nova,

Manuels. It was Father Morris's intention to not only care for the orphans under his care, but to train them in various trades so that they would be prepared to make their own way in life after leaving the orphanage. The new orphanage thrived and by 1889, there were 127 boys at the orphanage which was now self supporting with a shoe factory, a tailor shop and a bakery. Then tragedy struck. Four boys, sent out to drive home the orphanage cattle, drank from a stagnant pool and developed typhoid fever. The disease spread and sixty-five boys were stricken. The orphanage was quarantined. Father Morris and Dr. Keegan, a young doctor fresh from Ireland, nursed the sick boys. Thanks to the heroic efforts of Father Morris and Dr. Keegan only four boys died. They were buried together in a plot near the orphanage. However, Father Morris contracted the disease and fell a victim to it on August 1, 1989. After his death, the orphanage and school fell on hard times and was eventually closed. A momument to Father Morris still stands in Bannerman Park today.

Newfoundland Roman Catholic schools continued to operate under a denominational system, and the bishops and parish priests remained the educational leaders until the second half of the 20th century.

R.C. Cathedral (Basilica)

Chapter Sixteen

The Building of a Cathedral and More Politics

The Cathedral (Basilica) of St. John The Baptist:

The building of the Cathedral of St. John the Baptist—now the Basilica of St. John the Baptist—was one of the greatest monuments to the faith of the Irish Roman Catholics of Newfoundland. When Bishop Fleming, after long delays, finally secured a site, the whole Irish community, aided by their Protestant neighbours, cut and hauled a vast quantity of stone from Kelly's Island. They raised huge sums of money and devoted hours of free labour to bring Bishop Fleming's dream to fulfilment. It stands today as a monument to the faith and determination of those hardy souls who overcame all odds to build a strong and vibrant Irish community in Newfoundland.

The Building of the Cathedral:

The corner stone of the cathedral was laid in May of 1841 by Bishop Fleming, but he did not live to see the building completed. On January 6, 1850, knowing that his end was near, he celebrated the first mass in the unfinished edifice. He died on July 14 of the same year. Five years later on September 9, 1855, the building was consecrated by Bishop Thomas Mullock O. F. M., Fleming's successor. The cathedral was constructed of local stone from Kelly's Island and faced with cut limestone from Galway, Ireland and Dublin granite.

The consecration of the cathederal was an event to be remembered with pride by the Newfoundland-Irish. Three bishops and an archbishop from as far away as New York came to help in the celebrations, as did twenty-four priests of the various Newfoundland parishes. The Roman Catholic members of the House of Assembly were also there. At night every Irish house in St. John's was illuminated in honour of the great event. Built on a commanding site overlooking St. John's Harbour it remains a monument to the faith of the Irish immigrants who settled in St. John's.

Bishop Mullock and the Steamship Controversy:

Bishop Mullock, who succeeded Bishop Fleming in 1850, was a man of strong views who was very interested in the development of Newfoundland. In a letter to a St. John's newspaper in 1855, he supported a cross-country telegraph service for the island, and suggested the possibility of a submarine cable link with Europe.

Bishop Mullock was also very interested in obtaining a steamship for the Newfoundland coastal service. In 1860, while on a visit to New York, the bishop virtually made a contract to hire a steamer called the S.S. *Victoria* for the Newfoundland coastal servive. However, the government refused to honour the Bishop's unauthorized agreement and he dashed off a letter to the press accusing the government of "legalized robbery." He withdrew his support of the Kent administration and called on Catholics and Protestants to support the introduction of the steamship service. He followed up this attack with another attack on the granting of Poor Relief. In a letter to the governor he gave his opinion of the elected members and those who had elected them:

> The members in a great measure were choosen only as the
> representatives-beggers of a set of paupers, and he who

could get most flour was the best member. The whole system was one of robbery and demoralization on all sides, for the distribution of Poor Relief among the idle and the improvident and for political purposes is the worst species of political robbery, for it not only debases the distribution (if anything could do that) but debases and demoralizes the recipients nearly to the level of their corrupters.

The effect of the bishop's attack on the predominately Irish Catholic Liberal party was devastating. Strengthened by Bishop Mullock's denunciation, the Governor, Sir Alexander Bannerman, who had only been waiting for an opportunity to do so, dismissed the Liberal ministers and called on the Protestant opposition leader, Sir Hugh Hoyles, to form a new government.

However, the Liberal Prime Minister, John Kent, fought back and his motion that the dismissal of his government was a "gross act of treachery" was passed sixteen to twelve in the House. The governor then disolved the assembly and called a new election.

The prospect that he might have to deal with a new Protestant-led government forced Bishop Mullock to retract his former accusations about the Liberal Party. In a letter to the papers he denounced the election call and in an about face, called the Liberal Party the party of civilization and the vehicle through which the Catholic clergy, and they alone, had effected every improvement thus far made in Newfoundland." The policy of their opponents was that of enemies of Catholicism everywhere, to divide, conquer and enslave." He went on to say Roman Catholics must support the candidate chosen by their priests and not independent Catholic candidates. The new election, he declared, was merely an "Irish Landlord trick."[1] One journalist suggested that "Bishop Mul-

---

1   CO 194/165, Governor Bannerman to Newcastle, May 16, 1861 copy of Bishop Mullock's letter to the Record of March 21, 1861.

lock, staggered by the catastrophe he had helped to bring about, could not afford to mince words."

The Protestant Party led by Hoyles—supported by Governor Bannerman—hoped to elect four members in addition to those who had served in opposition in the former House of Assembly. This would give them a majority and they would form the government. In fact, the election saw Governor Bannerman and Bishop Mullock as political rivals in a fiercely contested election.

There was trouble in the four districts which had a large Irish-Newfoundland population: St. John's, Harbour Main, Harbour Grace and Carbonear.

St. John's:

In St. John's there were five nominations for the three seats. The Liberals were divided into two rival factions, "the priest's party" and the "natives party." One of those nominated was a Protestant merchant. However, after a priest addressed a political gathering, a mob attacked the business premises of the Protestant candidate but was repelled with gunfire by the occupants who were expecting an attack. As a result, the Protestant merchant, along with another independent Catholic, withdrew from the contest. The bishop's candidates were elected.[1]

Harbour Main:

At Harbour Main there were four Roman Catholic candidates for the two seats. Two candidates, Hogsett and Furey were supported by the bishop and Father Kieran Walsh of Harbour Main Parish. Two other candidates. Knowlan and Byrne were supported by a neighbouring parish priest. At that time, the electors of Salmon Cove (Avondale) had to go to Cat's Cove (Conception Harbour) to vote. On election day the men from

1   Gunn, *Political History of Newfoundland*, 1832-64, p.162.

Harbour Main, led by Father Kieran Walsh, accompanied the Salmon Cove men to Cat's Cove. The men from Cat's Cove assembled just outside their community with weapons, determined not to let the others enter their town.

The men from Harbour Main and Salmon Cove were determined that they would vote. In the ensuing melee, George Furey, a resident of Harbour Main, was killed and a number of others were wounded. The Harbour Main and Salmon Cove men retreated leaving the Cat's Cove men the victors. When the votes were counted Furey and Hogsett lost to Knowlan and Byrne. Despite this the Roman Catholic Returning Officer at Harbour Main gave, under duress, a certificate of return to Hogsett and Furey. However, he also endored the writ of return for Nowlan and Byrne saying that they had the majority of votes.[1]

Harbour Grace:

In the first election under Responsible Government the District of Harbour Grace returned one Roman Catholic and one Protestant member. However, as the district had a majority Protestant population Hoyles' Party hoped to elect two Protestant members. There had been trouble at the Harbour Grace elections in 1859 and 1860 and the governor sent over 100 soldiers to keep the peace on Election Day. However, despite the presence of the troops one of the Protestant candidates withdrew, and the magistrates of the town cancelled the election because they feared violence.

The St. John's Riot of May 13, 1861:

The election of 1861 gave the Hoyles party fourteen seats in a twenty-six member House of Assembly. The election return from Harbour Main was invalid, until it was decided who was legitimately elected, and an election would have to be held at

1 *Journal of the House of Assembly*, 1861, p.13.

Harbour Grace at a later date. When the House of Assembly opened on May 13, there was trouble, for Hogsett and Furey occupied the two seats for Harbour Main and refused to leave when challenged. Hogsett was removed by the police and Furey followed him out of the chamber.

Then a mob of about 2,000 persons assembled to harass the government members. They tried unsuccessfully to break into the House of Assembly, where according to Judge Prowse they were kept out by "a tall Irishman who put his back against the door and defended it against the whole excited rabble." The mood of the crowd then turned violent and they began to attack the business premises and homes of the friends and supporters of Knowlan and Byrne, the two legitimate elected members for Harbour Main.[1] When the destruction of property began, the magistrates called out the troops from the St. John's garrison. About ninety men under the command of Colonel Grant arrived on the scene and the Riot Act was read by Judge Little, but to no avail. The mob would not disperse. Several Roman Catholic priests attempted to persuade the crowd to go home, but were ignored. The mob grew bolder, stones were thrown at the soldiers and some of them attempted to drag Colonel Grant off his horse. The Colonel and his men endured these insults, but when a shot rang out from the crowd, Colonel Grant gave the order to fire. Three people were killed and twenty wounded, including Father Jeremiah O'Donnell who was shot in the ankle. A man named Patrick Myrick, who was assisting Fr. O'Donnell, was shot in the thigh.

At this crucial moment Bishop Mullock took command. The bells of the Roman Catholic Cathederal rang out and the rioters obeyed the summons of their bishop and crowded into the Roman Catholic cathederal to hear him speak. Dressed in full pontificals he told them in no uncertain terms

1 Prowse, *History of Newfoundland*, First Edition, p. 489.

to cease and desist and, raising the Host in the air, extracted a promise of peace. The riot was over and the crowd returned to their homes.

Destruction of Returning Officer's House at Harbour Main:

The riot was over in St. John's but 5 days later, on May 18, at Harbour Main, an angry mob surrounded the house of the Returning Officer and pulled it to the ground. They butchered his cattle and even threw the bread his wife had in rise into the ocean. Before attacking the house the mob cut the telegraph wires linking Harbour Main with St. John's, so news of the outrage did not reach the governor until the next day. He promply sent troops by a steamer to apprehend those responsible. A number were arrested and taken to St. John's. At their trial, the Returning Officer and his family could not be persuaded to testify against them and the jury found them not guilty. The governor was also informed that Father Kyran Walsh had been present at the destruction of the house, but had made no effort to protest the outrage. On June 25, an election committee of the House of Assembly pronounced Byrne and Nowlan duly elected and they took their seats.

First complaints of "Orangeism" in Newfoundland:

Hogsett and his colleagues now prepared a petitioned to the Queen for the removal of Governor Bannerman. The petition was brought to the Roman Catholic cathedral for a number of Sundays and collected 8,000 signatures including 10 Roman Catholic priests, two members of the House of Assembly and a number of members of the former Liberal government. The petition accused Governor Bannerman and Prime Minister Hoyles of setting up a reign of "Terror, Tyranny and Fraud." The petition was sent to the Limerick member of parliament who presented it to the Duke of Newcastle. He in turn presented it to the queen, but did not advise her on how to respond to it.

Back in St. John's, Governor Bannerman believed that the petition from Hogsett and allies was meant to show in Ireland that "Orangeism" was rampant in Newfoundland, despite the fact that there was no Orange Lodge in the island. He quoted from material being read in the ale houses in St. John's which suggested "that unless an inquiry was made into the 'Orange tyranny' Her Majesty might find she had lost the key to the St. Lawrence."

There was much anxiety about the delayed election in Harbour Grace which had been set for the fall. However, Governor Bannerman sent troops to that town and had a naval ship on stand-by in the area before and after the election. Bishop Mullock issued a pastoral letter calling for peace, and he informed the governor he was prepared to excommunicate anyone carrying or using weapons. The election went smoothly with two Protestant members being elected. The Hoyles party now had a majority government.

The Interdict on Cat's Cove (Conception Harbour)

Eleven men were charged in the Harbour Main-Cat's Cove fray, and were brought to trial in St. John's. They challenged having a Roman Catholic jury, saying they could expect no justice from members of the Bishop's Party. They asked for an all Protestant jury. The Protestant jury found them guilty and five were sentenced to twelve months imprisonment, the others to nine months. Bishop Mullock was outraged at the light sentence. Then Governor Bannerman pardoned the eleven offenders which further outraged Bishop Mullock. The Bishop issued a decree which laid an interdict on Cat's Cove:

> Having made the necessary enquiries we have been con-
> vinced of the truth of an outrage on Religion and humanity,
> perpetratd in Cat's Cove, by public rejoicing and hoisting
> of flags, not only in the Harbour, but at the place where

George Fury was murdered, on the return of "Convicts from St. John's jail". Brutal and savage as that act itself, this last act shows that the perpetrators are a disgrace to human nature and the place they inhabit is branded with the curse of Cain. Therefore invoking the Holy Name of God, etc., we ordain that no Mass be said, no Stations held, and no sacrament, unelss to the dying (and Baptism in the case of extream necessity) be administered in Cat's Cove, for the next twelve months, from this date. The church will remain closed for the same time.

We pray that God may enlighten the darkened under-standing, and soften the stony hearts of these people, that by sincere repentance they may escape the awful judge-ment which his judgement holds over them.[1]

Bishop Mullock was even more angry when his candidate, Mr. Hogsett, was defeated by a rival Catholic candidate in a St. John's by-election.

The Confederation Issue of 1864:

In 1864, Newfoundland was invited to send two delegates to the Quebec conference. Sir Frederick Carter the Prime Minister, and Sir Ambrose Shea the leader of the Opposition, were chosen to attend. They both came back supporting the idea that Newfoundland should join Confederation. The idea was discussed but it wasn't until the election of 1869 that the question of Confederation with Canada was put to a vote.

Irish Opposition to Confederation:

The election of 1869 was based on the Confederation issue. Sir Ambrose Shea, the most prominent Newfoundland-Irish Roman Catholic in public life, was in favour of union with Canada. He and Prime Minister Carter campaigned for the Roman Catholic Liberal Party on this platform. Charles Fox

---

1 Gunn, *Political History of Newfoundland*, 1832-1864, p.174.

Bennet, a Protestant merchant, led the fight for the the anti-confederate Protestant Conservatives. Strangely enough, the Newfoundland Irish and their priests opposed confederation. The Irish were afraid of heavy taxes and opposed to conscription. At Witless Bay, Sir Ambrose had to flee for his life when the women of the community went after him. At Placentia he was greeted by a mob and howled down when he tried to speak. He laid the blame for this reception on Father Condon, the Parish Priest of Placentia, who was an ardent anti-confederate. In the district of St. Mary's—nearly 100% Roman Catholic—where he was running, Sir Ambrose received only 100 votes. The anti-confederates won the day.

A New Roman Catholic Bishop for St. John's:

In March of 1869, Bishop Mullock died and a year later was succeded by Bishop Thomas J. Power, a County Wexford man. He was the last native born Irish priest to become bishop of St. John's.

Bishop Dalton of Harbour Grace diocese died a few months after Bishop Mullock and was succeded by the Reverend Enrico Carfagnini as the second bishop of Harbour Grace.

Bishop Carfagnini and The Bevevolent Irish Society of Conception Bay:

In 1814, a group of Irish-Newfoundlanders established the Benevolent Irish Society of Conception Bay with headquarters at Harbour Grace. It was fashioned on the St. John's B.I.S. and adopted the same rules as that society. Over the years the Conception Bay B.I.S. did much to help alleviate the distress of the poor in that area. Everything went well with the society until the appointment of Bishop Carfagnini in 1869. Bishop Carfagnini was an Italian priest who had come to Newfoundland as Principal of St. Bonaventures College and spoke very imperfect English.

His appointment did not sit well with the Irish clergy of

his diocese and relations became very strained when the bishop attempted to take control of the Benevolent Irish Society. In 1874 he ordered the executive of the society to give him full control of the society and its funds. The executive of the B.I.S.—secretly supported by many of the Irish clergy—refused his order. The bishop's response to the refusal was to issue an episcopal decree disolving the old society. Then, he established a new B.I.S. society with an executive appointed by himself.

The old executive declared the bishop had no authority over their society and rerfused to disband or hand over their funds or clubroom. Bishop Carfagnini responded by giving them fifteen days to obey his decree or face excommunication. As well any priest supporting them would immediately be suspended from his priestly duties.

The old executive of the B.I.S. and their supporters remained firm and refused to obey the bishop's order. He imposed the excommunication, but the people would not recognize his order of excommunication. Instead they bombarded Rome with letters and telegrams complaining of Bishop Carfagnini's actions. Cardinal Franchi, the Prefect of the Sacred Congregation at Rome, was astounded at the protest and summoned Bishop Carfagnini to Rome to explain his actions. From October 1875 until the spring of 1876, the Bishop remained in Rome pressing his case. The Irish Roman Catholic people of Harbour Grace continued to bombard Cardinal Franchi with protests about the bishop's conduct. In the spring of 1876, the Pope ordered the excommunication order lifted and ordered Bishop Carfagnini to leave the B.I.S. alone, as it was a lay and not a religious society. An advertisement in the *Harbour Grace Standard* by Cardinal Franchi made sure there would be no misunderstanding about the Pope's decision.

For six more years Bishop Carfagnini remained at Harbour Grace, then he again annoyed his Irish clergy by appointing an Italian priest to a senior parish that had fallen vacant. Again the letters and telegrams bombarded the Holy Office demanding the removal of the unpopular bishop. Rome had enough: Bishop Carfanini was raised to rank of Archbishop and appointed to the see of Gallioli in Italy.

On May 27, 1880, an ocean liner called in at Harbour Grace to take the bishop on board. On that day the legend of the Harbour Grace Prophecy was born.

It was reported that as the liner moved out of the harbour, Bishop Carfagnini stood on her deck and took a last look at the scene of his late episcopal labours. As the town began to fade from view he turned to those around him and prophesied that never again would the town of Harbour Grace prosper. Instead, it would fall slowly into oblivion and become little more than a ghost town. Bishop Carfagnini was succeed by a Bishop Ronald MacDonald from Pictou, Nova Scotia, and peace and harmony was restored to the diocese.

The Harbour Grace Affray of 1883:

This last and perhaps most bitter clash between the Roman Catholic Newfoundland Irish and the Protestant Newfoundland English occured at Harbour Grace. The occasion was the annual parade of the Loyal Orange Society. On December 26, 1885, about 450 Orangemen from Harbour Grace and the neighbouring communities of Bay Roberts, Spaniard's Bay and Carbonear assembled to attend service at the Methodist Church on Water Street, Harbour Grace. After service they began to parade through the town. However when they were near Pippy's Lane they were met by about 150 Roman Catholics from River Head who were determined that the Orangemen should not pass through Pippy's Lane from Harvey Street to Water Street. This area was supposed to be the territory of the Irish Roman Catholics. An argument ensued and soon shots were fired. In the fray that followed, five men died and seventeen were wounded.

The government sent a detachment of mounted police under the command of Head Constable John Sullivan to arrest those believed to be responsible for the deaths and woundings. A trial followed and all the arrested men were acquitted of the murder charges. Fourteen others were granted bail while waiting for the other charges against them to be heard. Five of the fourteen accused later had the charges against them dropped and they were released.

The Protestant community was outraged at the acquittal of the prisoners and a "General Protestant Union was formed" with John Rorke as president, to join together all the Protestants in Newfoundland for the protection of "Protestant Rights." However, this organization did not succeed in its aims and objectives and soon disbanded.

Fair Denominational Representation in Distribution of Offices:

The Harbour Grace Affray was the last major confrontation in Newfoundland between the Irish-Newfoundland Roman Catholics and the English-Newfoundland Protestants. In order to allay the suspicions of each party, the government adopted a policy that all religious parties should be fairly represented in the distribution of offices. This effectively helped to diminish the violent sectarianism that had been so evident in the colony since the granting of Representative Government in 1832.

Sir Ambrose Shea Appointed Governor of the Bahamas:

June 22, 1887, was a great day for the Newfoundland-Irish for on that day the St. John's *Evening Mercury* announced the appointment of Sir Ambrose Shea as Governor of the Bahamas. Sir Ambrose was the first native born Newfoundlander of Irish ancestry to be appointed to a vice-regal position. It was great news for the Newfoundland-Irish and on October 20, 1887, they gathered on the pier of the Allan agents to wish Sir Ambrose bon voyage.

The First Native Born Roman Catholic Bishop:

The year 1892 marked a another first for the Newfoundland-Irish for that year, the Reverend Michael Francis Howley, the son of a Tipperary immigrant was, consecrated as the first bishop of the diocese of St. George's. He was the first native born son to be appointed bishop in his own country. In 1895, on the death of Bishop Power, he was appointed bishop of the St. John's diocese, and in 1904 he was created archbishop. A historian, and writer, as well as a prelate, Bishop Howley made a great contribution to Newfoundland history.

Peace and Harmony:

By the turn of the century, there was peace and harmony in the island between the Irish Roman Catholics and the English Protestants. The denominational principle maintained in the Civil Service and the Education system removed the cause of friction and the two races, English and Irish, began to learn to live at peace and trust one another.

Canada's Newest Province

Sir Ambros Shea

Appendix

List of Irish Convicts Confined at the Signal Hill Camp.

Name	Age	Birth	Crime	Sentence	Place
Brosnahan Con	23	Tralee	robbery & Murder	Death*	
Burleigh John	19	Garahtown	theft	Transportation	C. Meath
Butler Will	27	Limerick	robbery & murder	death*	
Byrne John	22	Sargart	stole a coa	Transportation	C. Dublin
Byrne Tim	30	Mountrath	highway Robbery	Death*	C. Queens
Carey Darby	54	Callan	swindling	Transportation	C. Kilkenny
Carpenter Nick	25	Crambin	?	?	C. Dublin
Cashall James	23	Limerick	?	?	
Coyle John	21	Dublin	vagrant	Transportation	
Delaney Mick	22	Ballymore	theft	Transportation	Wicklow
Dempsey Matt	21	Clonshee	picking a lock	Death*	King's County
Delaney Mick	22	Ballymore	theft	Transportation	Wicklow
Duncan Tom	13	Kilcock	?	?	C. Meath
Ellis Sam	18	Tullow	vagrant	Transportation	C. Wicklow
Farrell John	14	Dublin	accomplice to rob a house	Transportation	
Fisher Robert	25	Dublin	robbery & murder	Death*	
Foley John	19	Dublin	pick pocket	?	
Franklin Will	23	Odennahaugh	theft	Transportation Escaped from camp August 22, 1789	C. Aramag
Flynn Mick	21	Cork	theft	Transportation	C. Cork
Gainpord John	18	Dublin	?	?	
Gibbons John	22	Dublin	attempted house break	Flogging & Transportation	
Grant James	19	Dublin	?	?	
Halfpenny Jim	23	Drogheda	?	?	
Hart Pat	14	Dublin	?	?	
Healey Pat	19	Dublin	?	?	
Hogg David	16	Edenacligh	stealing lead	Transportation	F. Farmanagh
Hurley Joh	22	Parteen	?	?	C. Clare
Kelly John	30	Athlone	coining	Death*	C. Rosecommon
Kelly Martin	20	Old Court	stealing wood	Transportation	Wicklow
Kelly Tom	20	Rathcoole	stealing 2 saddles	Transportation	Dublin
Keough John	22	Dublin	famous cart stealer	?	
Lacey Francis	41	Dormoth	sheep stealing	Transportation	Kildare

Name	Age	Birth	Crime	Sentence	Place
Lawler John	16	Dublin	?	?	
Lee Pat	24	Drogheda	?	?	
Leonard Pat	40	Cornegal	swindling	Death*	C. Cavan
Mahoney John	44	Mitcheltown	theft	Transportation	
McCarthy C.	55	Ballymurphy	?	?	Cork
McDermot Tom	20	Edgerstaron	stealing 1 lb tobacco	Transportation	C. Longford
McGuire James	25	Tanhouswater	forcible entry	?	C. Farmagh
Mooney Bart	29	Dublin	?	?	
Murphy John	13	Dublin	?	?	
Murray James	23	Drumclad	?	?	C. Monaghan
Neal Pat	40	Kilkenny	swindling	Death*	
Newenham Din	19	Dublin	accomplice with James Wyler in stealing man's watch	Death*	
Nugent Pat	40	Omagh	?	?	C. Tyronne
O'Brien Chas.	26	Rathfiland	pick pocket	?	C. Down
O'Neil John	20	Dublin	stealing vests	7 years Transportation escaped Aug. 22,/79	
Palleh Abraham	20	Cramlin	?	?	C. Monaghan
Parker Peter	20	Carlow	coining	Death*	C. Carlow
Pendergast M.	13	Dublin	?	?	
Reiley John	28	Cavan	coining	Death*	C. Cavan
Reiley James	28	Coat Hill	Highway robbery	Death*	
Ryan Martin	25	Humeward	burglary	Transportation	Wicklow
Sheridan Jim	40	Cornegall C. Cavan	stolen goods in house	Transportation	
Stewart Dan	19	Boltinglass	?	?	
Sullivan Mike	18	Bruff	pick pocke	Transportation	Limerick
Vance Lansht	40	Sheagh	?	?	C. Faramagh
Walpole Will	20	Cashell	?	?	Tipperary
Wyler W.	20	Donaghadee	stealing watches	Transportation	C. Down

* Death sentence was commuted to transportation.

The names of those who embarked on the *Elizabeth* were:

Males:

Bailey James
Brosnahan Con
Bryant Charles
Burke John
Butler William
Byrne John
Byrne Tim*
Cahill Tom
Carew Dan
Carpenter Nick
Connors Tom
Coyle John
Crook John
Delaney Mick
Dempsey Matt
Dunne Pat
Dunne Tom
Ellis Tom
Finn Mick
Fisher Robert
Fling Patrick
Foley Joe
Franklin William*
Gainford John
Grant John
Halfpenny John
Hart Patrick
Hagie David
Healey Pat
Horley John

Killan John
Kelly Mark
Kelly Tom
Lahey Tom
Leigh Pat
Leonard Pat
Linehan William
Linsay Tom
Mahoney John
Maney Bart
Mansfield John
McCarthy Charles
McCarthy John
McDornet John
McElles Dan
McGuire John
Moore James
Moore John
Mulloney Pat
Murphy James
Murphy Mick
Neale Pat
Neal John
Nugent Pat
Nugent John
Pendergast Nick
Pollate Abraham
Robinson Robert
Ryan Mike
Ryan Tom

Sales John
Shannon Tom
Smith John
Stirid Dan
Sullivan Nick
Sullivan Pat
Taylor Thomas
Thilson Will
Trilly John
Vinn John
Young Anthony
Warpole Will
Welsh John

* Tim Byrne and James Riley both died on August 13, 1789 at St. John's. Will Franklin escaped.

Females:

Ar Mary
Connoll Mary
Farrell Nancy

Kelly Judith
Maloney Mary
Watson Eleanor

Irish Volunteers for the Local Militia at Placentia in 1794

Barron Lawrence
Blackburn Josiah
Blanch Mike
Blanch Thomas
Breen Thomas
Byran James
Carroll Owen
Colbum William
Collins Cornelius
Collins John
Collins Sam
Collins Thomas
Collins William
Cook Charles
Couch John
Devine Pat
Devine William
Downs James
Fitzpatrick John
Foley James

Gibbons John
Gorman John
Grant Thomas
Green John
Green Robert
Hearne Philip
Hooper William
Hunt John
King Mick
Lambe John
Lambe John Jr.
Lambe William
Lee Daniel
Linnard Frank
Maclleroy John
Maddocke James
Masters William
McGrath Jerry
Miller Pat
Miller William

Mooney Pat
Mooney Robert
Mullowney Tom
Murphy Pat
Newman William
Nicolle Clement
Oakley James
Parnell Ambrose
Paul Harry
Payne Thomas
Peddle William
Power Edmond
Redmond William
Rogers William
Rose William
Squires James F.
St. Croix Charles
St. Croix John
St. Croix Richard.
Vicquers John
Vicquers Thomas
Walker James
Walsh James
Walsh Edmund.

A Typical Irish Planter's Estate in 1788:

Towards the end of the 18th century there were many Irish planters in Newfoundland. An inventory of the plantation of Robert Keating, an Irish planter of Little Placentia, (Argentia) gives an ideal of the typical value of the plantation of a successful Newfoundland-Irish Planter.

Inventory of the Plantation of Robert Keating
At Little Placentia, Newfoundland

A fishing room for three boats with a stage dwelling house thereon with a keeve, druges and barrows for a stage.

A garden at the end of a house occupied by James Colsdey, a garden and cow house on the Virgin Point, another garden adjoining thereto. 450 pounds.

3 cows and 1 yearling	valued at	48 pounds
1 mare, 2 years old		55
70, two hds salt, 6 leads, 6 old lines		5
An old shallop road, old rigging, 1 anchor		1 pound, 10s.
A shallop fit for a voyage		20
Total Value of Plantation		550 P. 10 S. 6d.

List of Persons Liscened to Keep Public Houses in 1797

Michael Little	John Widicomb
John Cox	Edmond Doyle
John Bolan	Michael Hanlon
Sarah Martin	Patrick Redmond
John Cahill	John Power
William Power	Thomas Murphy
Patrick Flannery	William Pendergast
Augustus McNamara	Dominic King
William McCarthy	George Shepherd
William Welsh	David Power

Patrick McDonald
Andrew St. John
Peter Lyons
Michael Mara
John Maher
John Flood
John Brophy.

Michael Welsh
John Nevean
Philip Harrahan
Daniel Delaney
Mark Codey
Michael Welsh

Some Early Interesting Court Cases in St. Mary's
The Witchcraft Libel Case

On October 8, 1819, a surrogate court was held at St.
Mary's and Mr. Glascock, assisted by the local magistrate Mr.
Phippard, sat in judgement. The most unusual case to appear
was that of Jane Haleran versus Catherine Walsh. The magistrate's report reads:

Petitioner (Jane Haleran) states defendant (Catherine
Walsh) has falsely accused her of witchcraft and prays for a
summons for defendant to appear before the court. A summons was granted accordingly for defendant to appear in
court on October 15, 1819 before Mr. Phillips Esq. magistrate
who is to examine into the merits of the case.

Mr. Phillips did not make it to St. Mary's, so, on November
26, 1819, the local magistrate, Mr. Phippard held a court to
decided on the charge of slander against Jane Haleran.
Despite being summoned to court, Mrs. Catherine Walsh did
not appear to face her accuser. In spite of her absence Mr.
Phippard proceeded with the case. The court record gives the
following account of the proceedings.

> This case came before William Glascock Esq. Surrogate but
> was deferred until the 15th of October by summons
> granted to the plaintiff. The parties appeared on November
> 26, plaintiff stated the defendant had accused her of witch-
> craft and when plaintiff came to see defendant at James
> McGrath's (next door) that the plaintiff went over to Peter's

River decidedly to take away the milk of a cow by force of witchcraft. Plaintiff produced two witnesses to prove her case.

Hugh Kiely Sworn:
States that he heard defendant say that she suspected no other person but the plaintiff for the loss of her cow's milk.

Ellen Peddle Sworn:
States that she heard defendant say—that she suspected no other person—but the plaintiff for taking away the milk from defendant's cow—but still she could not say that she did.

Another interesting case in 1819 dealing with the social problems of the time involved Ann St. Croix and her husband Benjamin. The case reads:

Ann St. Croix, a woman of 35 charged her husband Benjamin St. Croix, aged 77 with neglect and ill treatment for the last two years and prayed the court that he be compelled to provide support for her and her seven children. The parties not agreeing to live together—under order of the court—the defendant made an agreement to give up the use of his house and garden to the others and to pay 6 pounds at the end of the present season and 5 pounds per annum in future for the support of the children who were to be left in her charge.

The possible cause of the trouble between Ann and Benjamin become apparent a year later when Ann was again in court demanding child support from Edward Power of Trepassey for a child born July 17, 1822, of which she claimed he was the father. Power was ordered to pay child support.

Domestic service at St. Mary's could also be difficult for both the servant and her family as appears in the case of Mrs. James Butler versus Richard Critch.

Margaret Butler sworn and said:

My husband's name is James. I live at the Gaskiers. I recollect Sunday, August 6, when Richard Critch came into my house and demanded my daughter's Johanna's clothes. He had no right to make such a demand. She is servant to said Richard Critch. I refused to give clothes and then contrary to my wish he entered my sleeping-apartment. I told him I would proceed at law unless he desisted from entering my room. After searching and finding no clothes he seized my person and beat my head against the side of the house. He then went on the road and threatened to take my life before nightfall.

Johanna Butler was sworn and told how Critch had ill used her by kicking her and beating her on the flake. It was after such treatment that she left and went home.

Richard Critch was found guilty and fined 2 pounds and bound over to keep the peace.

Proclamation

William 1V by the grace of God of the United Kingdom and Great Britain and Ireland, King, Defender of the Faith; To All Our Loving Subjects In Our Island Of Newfoundland, Greetings:

Whereas on the 28th day of November last a warrant under the hand and seal of our Chief Justice of our said Island was issued for the apprehension of Michael Christopher (otherwise called Yetman), Patrick Tobin, Stephen Connors, Thomas Murray, Thomas Whelan, James Fagan the elder, John Bishop and Geoffery Quilty all of St. Mary's. in the Southern District of our said Island, fishermen charged upon oath before our said Chief Justice with having committed a riot at St. Mary's aforesaid,

AND WHEREAS it appears by the information of the peace officers charged with the execution of the said warrant and of other persons who were present that the peace officers were in the month of December last at St. Mary's aforesaid openly and violently resisted in the performance of their duty while endeavouring to apprehend the said offenders by a large number of armed men, inhabitants of St. Mary's aforesaid and that the peace officers were beaten and threatened with further violence if they persisted in endeavouring to execute the said warrant, whereby they were prevented from apprehending any of the said parties named in the warrant and were compelled to desist from any further attempt to perform their duty, and the said offenders do still remain at large in contempt of our authority and the laws of our said Island.

AND WHEREAS it is a high misprision and contempt of our ROYAL PREROGATIVE to resist lawful commands of our judges, justices, and other officers of justice or to be aiding or assisting in the rescue or escape of any persons charged with any offense against our laws or to neglect or refuse to assist any sheriff, Justice of the Peace, constable or other peace officer in the apprehension of any such offenders when thereto required by any of the said peace officers.

NOW THEREFORE KNOW YE that we do by this OUR ROYAL PROCLAMATION strictly charge and command the said Michael Christopher (otherwise known as Yetman), Patrick Tobin, Stephen Connors, Thomas Murray, Thomas Whelan, James Fagan the elder, John Bishop and Geoffery Quilty to surrender themselves to our officers and ministers of justice to be dealt with according to law. And we do further charge and command all our loving subjects to be aiding and assisting our sheriff of our Island and our Justice of the Peace and other peace officers in the apprehension of the said offenders and in bringing them to justice. AND lastly we do further command and strictly enjoin all persons throughout our said Island that they in no wise harbour, conceal comfort or in any manner be aiding or abetting the said offenders or any of them in their further resistance to our lawful authority upon pain of our highest displeasure and the punishment that shall await them.

Given under the GREAT SEAL of our said Island of Newfoundland.

Witness our trusty and well beloved Henry Prescott Esquire at St. John's in our said Island the 7th of May 1836, in the sixth year of our reign.

PETITION TO GOVERNOR PRESCOTT

THE HUMBLE PETITION OF THE UNDERSIGNED FISHERMEN OF ST. MARY'S IN THE SOUTHERN DISTRICT OF NEWFOUNDLAND
MOST HUMBLY SHOWETH:

(1) That from time immemorial the Beach of St. Mary's has been used as a commons by the people no rights of property thereof claimed or exercised by any individuals in the memory of the oldest inhabitant—used for repairing and careening boats, laying them up in winter and spreading nets in summer.

(2) It served as the only public path to Riverhead, and road for people of the Bay to reach the church and burial ground.

(3) The mound behind the beach not considered as private property—all used it for drying nets and seines—part of the hight ground was public cemetery and adjoining the cemetery the inhabitants built a church, but the building was blown down—a few years later a second church was built but this too blew down.

In the spring of 1834 William Fewer built a fish flake on part of the Beach—But in the grey of the morning Martin J. P. had the fence cut down, then immediately erected a flake along the entire length of Beach—depriving the people from their drying place.

A new church had been built on the mound back of the beach—Mr. Martin tried to get Reverend James Duffy to exchange this site for another place the property of Slade Elson. A poor site both wooded and wet—very inconvenient, the clergyman rejected the offer.

That after repeated requests the people went and cut off a portion of the flake that was considered on the commons—then in February 1935 they cut down the whole flake—no symptoms of riot or disorder.

Then Judge De Barres of the Southern Circuit held court at St. Mary's no criminal case presented.

In December several persons landed back of the Point and coming in secretly said they had been cast away at Trepassey, said they were in distress and put into St. Mary's for provisions. Later when they claimed to be the crew of the Colonial Yacht their authority was discredited, and they felt the poster was flawed.

On January 14, Dr. Fleming sent a letter telling them that they had been outlawed by a Proclamation and in compliance with his Lordship's advice they made instant preparation to leave for St. John's, arrived on Thursday and gave bail.

Asked to be tried in St. Mary's under the Southern Circuit not in St. John's, press had prejudged them.

Chief Sheriff turned them down, trial date set for July—middle of the caplin scull, all St. Mary's involved—seven married men out of the ten have fifty-five children.

Signed:

James Fagan X	John Bishop X
Patrick Tobin X	Geoffery Quilty X
Michael Christopher X	Stephen Connors X
Thomas Murray X	

The Indictment for Rex Versus James Duffy and others—Misdemeanour.

Nfld. St. John's, to wit

The jurors of our Lord the King, upon their oath, present that James Duffy, late of St. Mary's in the Southern District of the Island of Newfoundland, a Roman Catholic priest, Michael Christopher late of St. Mary's fisherman, otherwise called Michael Yetman, Patrick Tobin of the same place fisherman, John Bowen of the same place, fisherman, Stephen Connors late of the same place, fisherman. Thomas Murray late of the same place, fisherman, Thomas Whelan of the same place, fisherman, James Fagan the elder. of the same place, fisherman, John Bishop of the same place, fisherman, Geoffery Quilty of the same place, fisherman, together with divers other persons to the number of 60 to the jurors aforesaid yet unknown, being rioters, routers and disturbers of the peace of Our Lord the King on the thirteenth of January in the fifth year of the reign of our sovereign Lord William the fourth by the Grace of God etc. with force and arms did at St. Mary's aforesaid in the said district of the Island aforesaid unlawfully, riotously and roustously did begin to pull down, demolish and destroy a certain building erection and fish flake then and there situated in the possession of Robert Slade, John Elson, John Harrison, Mark Seager, and William Major, merchants and co-partners and did then and there at the same time and place aforesaid unlawfully , riotously pull down demolish and destroy a large portion and part of said building erection and fish flake to wit 100 feet in length and 24 in breadth and other wrongs to said Robert Slade, John Elson, John Harrison. Mark Seager and William Major and there did the great damage in contempt of Our Lord the King and his Laws to the evil example of all others in like cases offending and against the peace of our said Lord the King His Crown and dignity.

I certify that the foregoing is a true copy of the original Indictment remaining of Record in my office, St. John's, 28th., of December 1836.

A True Bill
Robert Job—Foreman
H. J. Boulton—Chief Justice.

Bibliography

Books

Anspach, Louis Rev., *A History of Newfoundland*, London, 1827.

Banks, Joseph, *Joseph Banks in Newfoundland and Labrador*, ed. A. M. Lysaght, London. 1971

Birkenhead, Lord, *The Story of Newfoundland*, London, 1920.

Bonneycastle, Richard Sir, *Newfoundland in 1842*, London, 1842.

Centenary Volume of the Founding of the Benevolent Irish Society, St. John's, 1906

Byrne, Cyril, J., *Gentlemen-Bishops and Faction Fighters*, St. John's, 1984.

Byrnes, John M., *The Paths To Yesterday*, Boston, 1931

Cell, Gillian T., *English Enterprise in Newfoundland 1577 -1680*, Toronto, 1969.

Chappell, Edward, Lt., *Voyage of His Majesty's Ship Rosamond to Newfoundland, London 1818.*

Connolly, R. J., *A History of The Roman Catholic Church in Harbour Grace*, St. John's 1986.

English, L. E. F., *Historic Newfoundland*, Montreal, 1967.

Devine & Lawton, *History of King's Cove*, St. John's, 1944.

Fay, C. R., *Life and Labour in Newfoundland*, Cambridge, 1956.

Galgay, Frank, *A Pilgrimage of Faith*, St. John's 1983

Gunn, Gertrude, *The Political History of Newfoundland 1832-1864*, Toronto, 1966.

Harvey, M., Rev., *A Short History of Newfoundland*, London, 1890.

Harvey M. Hatton, J., *Newfoundland*, London 1883.

Head, Grant, *Eighteenth Century Newfoundland*, Toronto, 1976.

Hibbs R., *The Newfoundland Road Booster*, St. John's, 1924.

Horwood, Harold, *Newfoundland,* Toronto, 1969.

Howley, Michael Rt. Rev., *Ecclesiastical History of Newfoundland* Boston, 1888.

Hunt, Edmund, Rev., *Aspects of the History of Trinity,* St. John's, 1981.

Innis, Harold, *The Cod Fishery,* Toronto, 1954.

Jukes, J. B., *Excursions In and About Newfoundland* (2 Vol) London, 1842.

Lounsbury, Ralph, *The British Fishery in Newfoundland,* 1634-1763 (Reprint Ed.) Hamden 1969

Maloney Queen, *Trail Wanderings,* St. John's, 1994.

Manion John, *Irish Settlement in Eastern Canada*, Toronto, 1974.

Moyles, R. G., *"Complaints is many and Various, but the odd Divil likes it,"* Toronto, 1975

Mosdell H. M., *When was That?*, St. John's 1922.

Murphy James, *The Colony of Newfoundland*, St. John's, 1925. *Customs of the Past*, St. John, 1918.

Murphy, Michael, *Pathways Through Yesterday*, St. John's, 1976.

Murray, Jean, *The Newfoundland Journal of Aaron Thomas*, Don Mills, 1968

O'Neill, Patrick, *An Outline History of Conche*, Conche, no date of publication.

O'Neill, Paul, *The Oldest City*, Erin, Ontario, 1975 *A Seaport Legacy*,Erin, Ontario, 1976

Pedley, Charles Rev., *The History of Newfoundland*, London, 1863.

Prowse, D. W. *A History of Newfoundland*, London 1895.

Reeves John, *A History of the Government of the island of Newfoundland*, London, 1793.

Rodgers J. D., *A Historical Geography of Newfoundland*, Vol, V, Oxford, 1911

Rowe, Frederick W., *Education and Culture in Newfoundland*, Toronto, 1976.

Seary, E. R., Place *Names of the Avalon Peninsula*, Toronto, 1971.

Smallwood, J. R., *The Books of Newfoundland*, (6 volumes) St. John's 1967

Smallwood J. R. etc. *The Encyclopedia of Newfoundland* (5 volumes) St. John's (1981-1994)

Smith, Harry, J., *Newfoundland Holiday*, Toronto, 1952.

Toque, Philip Rev., *Newfoundland as It Is In 1877*, Toronto, 1878

Webber, David, *Skinner's Fencibles*, St. John's, 1964.

Wicks,E. Rev. *Six Months of a Newfoundland Missionary's Journal*, London, 1836.

Articles

McCarthy, Michael J., *A History of Placentia*, Arts & Letters Publication, 1973.

The Irish In Newfoundland, Arts & Letters, Publication 1974.

Kinsella, Joseph, *Tilting Expatriate*, Volume 11.

Nemec, Thomas, "Irish Emigration to Newfoundland," *Newfoundland Quarterly* Volume 1V, July, 1972.

Shortis, H. F. "Fireside Stories," *Commercial Annual, Chriastmas Number*, St. John's, 1921

Other Government and Private Documents

Alberti Papers, C. O. 195/2

Calendar of State Papers, 1675

Colonial Papers Vols. XX11, XXXV, XXXV111

Colonial Letterbooks, 1749-1831

C. O. 194/3,f, 194/7, 194/25, 194/37, C. O. 194/38, 194/42, C. O. 195/13, C. O. 196/13,

Court Records for Ferryland, 1777-1790.
for St. Mary's 1819
for Fortune Bay, 1798-1812

Incoming Correspondence, S-2-2vp., 54 s-2,19 s-2,24,

Letterbook, Saunders and Sweetman, Letterbook, 1788,PANL

Index

Edwards Governor: 45
Elizabeth: 94, 97
Elford Lieut. Governor: 94
Escaped Irish Convicts: 96
Early Irish Settlers: 143
Early Irish Schoolmasters: 177
Ewer Thomas Father: 88, 128

F

Falkland Lord: 2,3,
Famine Ship: 119
Ferryland: 50, 88, 91, 122
Fewer Wm.: 145
Finn General: 126
Fitzpatrick Ambrose Father: 89
Fleming M.A. Bishop: 156,157,158,159,163,165,166, 167,168,170,171,172, i74, i75 178, 179, 180
Flip: 64, 67
Fogo: 87, 113,
Ford Thomas: 6
Franciscan Monks: 179, 180
Furey George: 190, 193

G

Galway: 186
Garland Magistrate: 35
General Protestant Union: 197
Glenly Lord: 154, 155
Gower Governor: 113

Grace Thomas: 169
Grant Colonel: 190
Greenspond: 25, 33

H

Harbour Breton: 60, 121
Harbour Grace: 2, 13, 35, 36, 37, 42, 49,70,91, 120, 129,163, 164, 188, 190, 194
Harbour Grace Affray: 196, 197
Harbour Grace Standard: 195
Harbour Main: 23, 64, 120, 188, 189, 192
Hayman Robert: 2
Heart's Content: 4
Hiberian Chronicle: 50
Hogan Wm.: 127
Hogan Timothy: 137, 138,139,163
Hogsett Mr.: 190, 193
Holloway Governor: 111
Holy Cross School: 182
Holyrood: 120
Howley Michael Bishop: 198
Hoyles Hugh Sir: 187, 189, 192
Hurley Constable: 151, 152

I

Ireland's Eye: 3
Irish Convict Ship: 93
Irish Frays; 67, 68, 69, 70, 75, 76, 77, 78

Irish Immigration: 45, 116,120, 121
Irish in Bonavista Bay: 114
Irish in Fortune Bay: 112, 113
Irish in Labrador: 58
Irish Merchants: 87
Irish on the Cape Shore: 114
Irish Papists: 48
Irish Ladies in Court: 80
Irish Soldiers: 5
Irish Youngsters: 59, 60, 61

K

Katen Michael: 37
Keegan Dr. 183
Keene Wm. Magistrate: 27, 28, 29, 30,31, 33, 34, 35, 65
Keene Wm. Jr.: 29, 33
Keene's store: 80
Kelly's Island: 185
Kennedy John: 33, 34
Kennedy Terrence: 40
Kent John: 135, 136, 163, 186, 187
Kerry: 1
Kilkenny: 64
Kilkenny Doones: 63, 125
King's Cove
King's Cross P.E.I. : 161
Kitchon Wm: 20
Knowlan Pat: 75